V

ABOUT

BRITAIN

For Richard Girling

WILD
ABOUT
BRITAIN

A lifetime of award-winning nature writing

BRIAN JACKMAN

FOREWORD BY
SIMON BARNES

ILLUSTRATIONS BY
JONATHAN TRUSS

BRADT

First published in book form in the UK in October 2017 by

Bradt Travel Guides Ltd
IDC House, The Vale, Chalfont St Peter, Bucks SL9 9RZ, England
www.bradtguides.com

Print edition published in the USA by The Globe Pequot Press Inc,
PO Box 480, Guilford, Connecticut 06437-0480

Text copyright © 2017 Brian Jackman
Illustrations copyright © 2017 Jonathan Truss
Edited by Rachel Fielding
Copy-edited by Caroline Taggart
Designed and typeset from the author's files by Dataworks and Ian Spick
Cover design by Pepi Bluck
Cover photograph: *Whooper swans (Cygnus cygnus) in flight, Caerlaverock WWT, Dumfries and Galloway, Scotland, UK. January.* Copyright © 2017 Danny Green/2020VISION/naturepl.com

This collection is drawn and adapted from articles previously published in *The Sunday Times*, the *Daily Telegraph* and *The Countryside in Winter* – please see acknowledgements.

ISBN: 978 1 78477 067 9 (print)
e-ISBN: 978 1 78477 532 2 (e-pub)
e-ISBN: 978 1 78477 433 2 (mobi)

British Library Cataloguing in Publication Data
A catalogue record for this book is available from the British Library

Production managed by Sue Cooper and Jellyfish Print Solutions; printed in the UK
Digital conversion by Dataworks

Contents

FOREWORD

SIMON BARNES

Simbajack

It's always good when Brian Jackman comes to Norfolk. For a start, it means we can talk lion, and that's not a conversation you get every day. Not in this country, anyway. I had some new stories to tell him, and I was damn sure he'd have some new ones for me, because he always does.

We crossed the River Yare on the groaning, clanking chain-ferry, and entered the pub that lies so considerately on the far side. We ordered pints and sandwiches and decided that it was warm enough for the first outside drinks of the year. An adventure indeed.

Let the lions begin.

The way the matriarch called the entire pride into action, one by one, and took them off into the dusk in pursuit of dinner. The night the same pride organised the perfect cooperative hunt right in front of us: blockers and chasers and catchers and all. The thrilling sight of lions when you're on foot: no longer an observer but prey.

I have spent a lot of time with lions; Brian has spent more. I have a lot of good lion stories; Brian has more and better. His manner is quiet and gentle, his sense of humour considerable but subtle and unraucous. We talked of Africa, the big adventure, walking with elephants and buffalos, wading rivers with crocodiles, and those long black nights in your hut or your tent surrounded by the music of lions.

Years ago Brian spent entire seasons with the Marsh Pride of the Maasai Mara, and wrote about them and their ways: *Simbajack*, his Swahili cognomen, meaning lion-man. Yet it's clear from a single second's acquaintance that Brian has no wish to challenge the lions for bush-skills, or to hunt them down, or even to identify with their ferocious way of life. There is no relish for violence in his love for lions.

He's not out there trying to prove his manhood: he just likes lions. He loves their wildness, their beauty, their hectic ad-hoc social lives. He loves above all the way that lions make humble people of us all: teaching us that that we humans are just one more mammal in the intricate ever-fragile web of life.

As we talked, pioneer swallows fizzed over the reeds at belly-tickling height. We could hear the soft murmuring of a sedge warbler, warming up for the big spring sing. A butterfly, a brimstone, was savouring the floral baskets that hung from the pub.

This too is a Jackman landscape. It's not just about the exotic and the dangerous and glamorous: it's also about what lies just beyond your front door. Our talk turned to England: he spoke of the peregrines he sees so often in Dorset and I spoke of marsh harriers. Was the female on eggs yet? Were there good views of hunting males?

And there across the river, low over the reeds, the classic wobbling silhouette of a marsh harrier on a hunting run, a male – we both had bins, obviously – in his three glorious colours. In 1971 there was just one breeding pair of marsh harriers in this country, now there are many, so rejoice.

Our damp and crowded island is also full of wonders: and here is a book full of them. Brian responds to the remaining wild places of Britain with the same quiet love that he has for the lions who have roared their way through his life.

Love is only the starting point of course. There's also the deft craftsmanship, the confident, unshowy use of language, the uncluttered understanding of what makes a tale and how best to tell it. It's there in the sympathetic ear he has for local sages and the people who are part of our great landscapes, allowing them their say, allowing the reader to listen. It's about craftsmanship: for it is craftsmanship that allows the love to come through and be shared.

Brian brings unfamiliar landscapes to life and allows you to share them, in sweltering days, in days of bitter chill, in days when the rain trickles down your neck and yet you daren't leave because the next wonder may come along in the very next minute. He also takes you to your favourite and familiar landscapes and allows you to see them for the first time all over again: and all by letting the landscape speak for itself. That's Brian's secret for you: he's the man who listens to landscapes.

The ferry clanked and chugged its way back and across, back and across, bringing cars and one vast shining Harley-Davidson. A few early stinkboats played dodge-the-ferry. We talked of whales and bears and of the small brown birds with sweet voices that welcome in the spring back here. Lions, warblers, butterflies, humans: we're all one, you know. The next couple of hundred pages will make that very clear.

Introduction

A Passion for Nature

How do you become obsessed by the wonders of the natural world? In my case I was lucky. Although my family lived in suburban Surrey, my father worked for what was then the Southern Railway, and one of his perks was a limited number of free tickets that enabled him to take us to Cornwall every summer.

One year, when I was no more than four years old, we stayed at Polurrian Cove on the Lizard Peninsula, and if I close my eyes I can still conjure up the vision of a shallow stream dribbling down to the beach, a jungle of flag iris, and a moorhen strutting between the stems on its outsize feet. Perhaps it was the colours that burned themselves indelibly into my young mind: the yellow flags, the moorhen's scarlet sealing-wax bill, the over-arching blue of the Cornish summer sky. Whatever it was, while the rest of the holiday was soon forgotten, that random snapshot has remained with me as one of my earliest childhood memories.

Growing up during Hitler's war made for an unusual childhood. I was five years old when the war broke out, and at infant school when the sirens moaned we filed out of class to sing *Run Rabbit Run* in the air-raid shelters while the Luftwaffe's squadrons roared overhead to drop their bombs on London.

Strangely, I don't think it ever occurred to me that Britain might lose the war. We just tightened our belts, learned to live with the sirens' banshee wail and looked forward to the days when we might once again feast on half-forgotten pre-war treats such as ice cream and bananas.

Bread, sugar, margarine, everything was rationed. Yet I never felt deprived. To feed his family my father dug up our lawn to grow potatoes. There was also a henhouse full of Rhode Island Reds to relieve the wartime diet of dried eggs that tasted like distemper, and a white rooster with the patriotic name of Winston, whom we ate for Christmas.

The years passed. The seasons went around in a whirl of schoolboy crazes. In autumn there were conkers. In winter, on days when frost flowers blossomed on the insides of my bedroom window, we made slides in the street outside, skidding down our suburban pavements until they shone like glass.

But summer was the golden time. Released from school in mid-afternoon, my friends and I would head for Nonsuch, the park that stood at the end of the road. This had once been the site of a great palace built by Henry VIII and subsequently demolished to pay off the gambling debts of the Countess of Castlemaine, into whose hands it had passed the following century. But of course we knew nothing of this. Instead, enclosed by fleets of blowsy elms, its unshorn meadows were our prairies, its hawthorn hedgerows our African savannas. In one field a landmine had fallen, blowing a deep crater in the clay that quickly filled with rain; and nature, always swift to exploit a niche, soon transformed it into a wildlife haven. (Years later, talking to the conservationist Dr David Bellamy, I discovered that he and I used to catch newts from this same pond.)

Nonsuch was the perfect adventure playground where I swung like Tarzan through the trees, made Robin Hood bows from young ash staves and built Apache dens among the cow parsley, but it wasn't the real countryside. This I knew because of those annual trips to Cornwall, which in those days seemed as exotic as the

Mediterranean. Going there was like travelling out of England into a foreign country where people spoke with an alien burr and called you 'my handsome'.

Across the Tamar the magnificent steam locomotives of the GWR ('God's Wonderful Railway') hauled us over echoing viaducts into a thrilling land of granite moors and foxglove lanes where the wind sang in the telephone wires as we clambered down to a sea so blue it might have been the Aegean. As we only went to Cornwall in summer, it seemed to be a place where the sun always shone, where palm trees grew and basking sharks cruised beneath the cliffs. Bathed in the dazzling Atlantic light, everything seemed twice as colourful: the painted boats, the pink hydrangeas – even the waves themselves as they thundered on Porthmeor sands or boomed in the bottle-green coves beyond Zennor.

Of course, we could never afford to stay for more than a fortnight. But one day, when the Blitz was at its height and the V-one 'buzz bombs' rained down on London, I became an evacuee and went to live on a farm near Bude. There, no sirens disturbed the deep West Country hush. I fell asleep to the hooting of owls in the woods and awoke to the triumphant clamour of a dunghill cockerel to begin a new life in an unchanged world of oil lamps and stone-flagged floors in which water, cold and pure, was drawn from a mossy well in the yard.

For two years I never went to school. Instead I fed the pigs their daily slops, hunted for hens' eggs in the nettle beds and learned to milk the cows by hand, leaning my forehead against their warm flanks while swallows twittered in the rafters and the pail foamed white between my knees.

Every Sunday we went to church, rumbling down the lanes in a painted wagon pulled by Punch, the farm horse. At ploughing time it was my job to hold him by the nose, leading him across the stubble as gulls boiled in our wake over each fresh-turned furrow.

As for friends, there were no fellow evacuees of my own age to play with, but I did not care. With the insatiable curiosity of small boys, I amused myself by running wild in the woods – looking for thrushes' nests, relieving my constant hunger by finding wild strawberries or picking blackberries until my hands turned purple.

It was, I suppose, an unhappy time for an eight-year old, alone and far from home, but its magic haunts me still. I did not know it then, but I had belonged, albeit briefly, to a way of life that has since followed the heavy horse into oblivion. Hardship there was, heartache and cruelty, but beauty and wonder, too, and the awakening of a love of all things wild that has stayed with me to this day.

When at last I returned to Surrey, speaking with an accent so broadly Cornish that even my parents could scarcely understand me, the war was drawing to its close. Another summer was just beginning and home had never seemed more welcoming.

In my absence, time had healed the scars of war. Weeds and garden flowers ran riot amid the rubble, transforming bombsites into rampant jungles of raspberry canes and dense thickets of willowherb in which, sometimes, as in the ruins of a lost city, I would stumble across a back-garden statue or a marble sundial half-choked in hogweed. And over all, like a cheap perfume, hung the cloying scent of mauve-flowering buddleia bushes.

It was the summer of the great invasion; not by Rommel's panzers but by swarms of butterflies. In the park, where trenches had been dug across the open fields to prevent German warplanes landing, thousands of tortoiseshells now sunned themselves on the tall thistles that had sprung unbidden from the disturbed clay.

I grew up with my cousin, Peter Grant; a year apart in age, as children we were inseparable. Even at that tender age, the budding scientist was apparent in his approach to the natural world. He went on to become a professor at Princeton, renowned for his lifelong study of Darwin's finches in the Galapagos, while I went down a different path and became a writer. Yet at that time we were united in our passion for catching butterflies and collecting hawk-moth caterpillars from roadside hedges, which we kept in jam jars until they pupated.

As the summer advanced, clouds of migrant butterflies – peacocks, painted ladies, red admirals and clouded yellows – poured across the Channel to settle on the bombsite buddleias, where they clung in clusters, drinking in the nectar with watch-spring tongues until they were too drunk to fly.

Today the suburbia I knew – bombsites, air-raid shelters, elm trees and all – has become part of a sepia world as remote to me as Tudor England. In Dorset where I live now my garden still attracts its share of red admirals. But whenever I return to my suburban roots, today scarcely recognisable with their carports and loft conversions, my mind runs back to those butterfly years when the sun shone and the buddleia flowered and summer seemed as if it could never end.

For as long as I can remember I had been a voracious reader, and by the time the war was over my mother had introduced me to Henry Williamson's countryside classic, *Tarka the Otter*. Set in my beloved West Country, it became my constant companion and I still have the dog-eared original into whose pages I would escape whenever suburbia became too claustrophobic. Later I would have the pleasure of meeting Williamson, once at a party given by the writer and broadcaster Kenneth Allsop, and again at Allsop's funeral in 1973 when, eyes blazing like an Old Testament Prophet, he read out a valedictory poem in his frail old man's voice. But that is jumping the gun.

Not until I was fifteen did I visit Europe for the first time, and even then it was only as far as Paris, accompanied by Cousin Peter and his father. My first independent trip abroad came about seven years later. By then I had completed two years' national service in the Royal Navy, and set off again with my cousin, only this time without my uncle to chaperone us.

For reasons I cannot remember we had chosen to head for the Costa Brava. Maybe the name – the Wild Coast – intrigued us. Anyway, we travelled by train down to Figueres in Catalonia and then by country bus to Rosas on the coast. Of course, this was a Costa Brava as yet hardly touched by the great post-war travel boom, and Rosas itself was still an authentic fishing village, of a kind so vividly described by Norman Lewis in *Voices of the Old Sea*.

By now I had joined *The Sunday Times* as a travel writer after an undistinguished career that had begun as a Fleet Street messenger boy. That was in 1970, when I became the lowest-paid journalist on the paper, but I did not care about the money. What mattered was that under Harold Evans, its great campaigning editor, *The Sunday Times* had become the most exciting newspaper in Britain and its travel pages were second to none.

Somehow I survived my baptism into the frantic world of Fleet Street – largely because I was so fortunate in my choice of sympathetic colleagues. Among those who used to subedit my copy was Ian Jack, who later became editor of *Granta*, and who once famously complained to me that he was 'merely the middle seven letters of my name'.

And so, for the next twenty years, *The Sunday Times* became my ticket to see the world. There were no limits; I went everywhere, from the Falkland Islands to Everest Base Camp, tracking tigers in the teak forests of Madhya Pradesh and searching for grizzlies in the North Yukon. But it was Africa that stole my heart away. Having seen my first wild lions in Kenya's Maasai Mara national reserve and heard them roaring at the dawn, I knew that I would have to return, although never in my wildest dreams did I imagine that over the next four decades I would spend the best part of four years under canvas in the African bush.

Yet for all the allure of those endless savannas and their teeming herds of game, I could never envisage living anywhere else except here in Britain, wrapped around by the changing seasons and much-loved landscapes that have shaped my life and given it a sense of purpose. Even in winter, when others may yearn for the warm south, I rejoice in the pleasures that keep me rooted at home when the leaves are down. In short, there is nowhere I would rather be.

So much of Britain is now a wasteland, wrecked and polluted beyond recall, with wildlife everywhere at risk. In my lifetime more than half the biodiversity of the UK has been lost and the rate of attrition continues unabated. In 2016 the State of Nature report, compiled by fifty-three country-wide wildlife organisations, warned that one in six of our wild species is in danger of disappearing – mostly due to intensive farming.

In Dorset where I live the cuckoo no longer heralds the return of spring, and many of the fields in this most rural of English counties are a beautiful illusion, emerald deserts devoid of life. Yet miraculously, out there beyond our sprawling cities and six-lane highways, you can still catch the pulse of an older, emptier Britain of heather moors and Pennine hay meadows, kingcup marshes and salmon pools, in which our finest landscapes and last wild places are now cherished as holy ground where, against all the odds, the nation's wildlife has survived.

Over the past forty years it has been my privilege and my joy to spend time in these sacred places, often with a view to seeking out the spectacular species that still inhabit them. This book is a result of those journeys: a celebration of the treasures our countryside offers, and a plea not to let them disappear.

Brian Jackman

West Milton, Dorset

September 2016

HOME GROUND

*As ever the gigantic hulk of Eggardon filled the sky, a green-skinned
swordfish lunging to impale Powerstock's shoal of cottages. Gulls soared
casually over the old smugglers' passes. A kestrel skimmed over the dale
lapped by surging bog oaks at the edge of King John's chase. My eye
wandered to the hanging wood where badgers' pads pulp the bluebell
stems like grape-treaders, across the brackeny dell where a vixen always
cubs, past the barn owls' home in the crumbled lime kiln, towards my
own village where the mill, and its flash of streams and wagtails, were
hidden in the enwrapping land.*

from In the Country *by Kenneth Allsop*

My Dorset

West Milton, August 2016

When I first came to Dorset, I used to wake to the sound of cows being driven down the lane after milking, the clatter of hooves and the slap of cowpats hitting the tarmac. Now the farm and its cows are no more. The farmer and his wife have gone, along with the barn owls that floated over the meadows at dusk, but the dawn chorus is as loud as ever. At first light, windows open, I can still hear it spilling down the valley: blackbirds, song thrushes, wrens and chaffinches – all singing fit to burst.

I grew up in suburban Surrey, surrounded by a sea of rooftops, but even before I was ten years old I knew that one day I would live in the West Country. As a boy I thought it would be Cornwall, where my parents spent their summer holidays, but that was before I discovered Dorset.

I had hitchhiked down from Surrey to meet a Royal Navy shipmate from my national service days. It was May, when the hills around Beaminster are as green as only Dorset hills can be. The old-fashioned fields glittered with buttercups. The cider orchards were in blossom, the cuckoos were calling and I thought I had never seen anywhere quite so quintessentially English.

The years went by and I bought a tumbledown cottage for a song – you still could in those days – and moved to Powerstock, lost in the hills northeast of Bridport. What I had stumbled on was a backwater on the way to nowhere, buried among hills too steep to plough, hemmed in by medieval lynchets, threaded by bluebell lanes and hollow ways so deep in places they almost shut out the sky. At first it was just a weekend bolthole, but later it became my permanent home. My daughter went to the village school and I knew there was no going back.

As for the village itself, it is pretty but not self-consciously so. It has a pub (Victorian), a castle mound (Saxon) and a real *Cider with Rosie* village school. At its centre, where five lanes meet, stands the Church of St Mary, with its crooked Norman chancel arch and a gilded weathercock slowly turning in the wind on its yellow Ham-stone tower. The churchyard is an ancient silence of sombre yews and leaning headstones. When I first came to live here it was the abode of Lazarus, a one-eyed tomcat who lived in a sepulchre and emerged at night to make sleep impossible with his amorous yowling.

Those were the days when barn owls hunted over the hay meadows, when colonies of house martins still nested under the eaves of the Three Horseshoes, and the old men sinking their pints inside spoke with such a broad Dorset burr that I could understand only one word in three.

During the week I had to go to London, where I worked as a journalist. But when Friday came I could hardly wait to catch the train to Dorchester and then drive westward, following the sun down the Roman Road to Eggardon, the giant hill fort that sits astride the geological frontier where the chalk downs of the South Country end and the true West Country begins.

From here it is downhill all the way. Plunge down the burrowing lanes and the landscape changes before your eyes, welcoming you with a flourish of ferns and the unmistakable smell of wild garlic until the village appears in the last of the light.

For thirty years, until I moved a couple of miles further down the valley, Eggardon filled my kitchen window, a billowing cloud of grassy limestone starred with flocks of grazing sheep. Seen from the village it looks huge, a displaced chunk of the Pennines that has no right to be here, a monument to Dorset's enduring nature. Even today I can still see its reassuring presence from the end of my garden, watching over our little valley.

Upon its summit, 830 feet above the sea, where the skylarks sing among the clouds, nothing changes. 'As old as Eggardon' goes the local saying. Until recently a solitary thorn tree stood on the top, ringed by ramparts raised in the Iron Age. Isaac Gulliver, an eighteenth-century smuggler turned MP, planted it as a day-mark for ships beating into Lyme Bay with contraband cargoes of French silk and brandies, and on a summer evening, when the sea turns to silver and the West Country light is as sharp as cider, you can see as far as Dartmoor.

This is not Thomas Hardy's Wessex, still less the genteel world of Jane Austen. Its literary heroes belong to more recent times – to the spirit of John Fowles on the Cobb at Lyme Regis, and above all to Kenneth Allsop, the writer and broadcaster who lived in the Georgian mill in West Milton.

'There is nowhere like it,' declared Allsop, whose book *In the Country* describes to perfection its 'tumbled anarchy of hills', and the feeling of being 'swallowed in the remoteness and antiquity of the land'. His words, written more than thirty years ago, still hold true today.

Everywhere, wildlife burgeons. Badgers rampage through my garden. Orange-tip butterflies waver among the cuckooflowers. When May comes, Abbotsbury Swannery is heaving with cygnets, and only a few miles farther west the peregrine falcons will be raising their young on the teetering cliffs of the Jurassic Coast.

What I came to think of as my Dorset is confined to the county's westernmost corner. It has no official boundaries: only the crumbling sea cliffs, thick with fossils, from Abbotsbury to Lyme Regis. Inland it melts away somewhere just north of Beaminster. That is the big picture. But the epicentre falls within a five-mile radius of Powerstock. For me this is the magic circle, a rumpled, tumbling green-gold land of secret combes and sensuously rounded plum-pudding hills. In pure landscape terms it's the crème de la crème, and the only place I know that still reminds me of the vanished countryside of my childhood holidays.

But my Dorset was never just a brief summer-holiday fling. To love a place truly you must know it in all its seasons. When the swallows have gone, when the hills vanish behind grey walls of drizzle and the entire county is as sodden as an unsqueezed sponge, it is time for autumn pilgrimages to Lewesdon, the county's highest hill, where the beechwoods seem to glow as if lit from within, or a long walk through the roadless valleys around Loscombe and Poorton, where buzzards sail over the dying bracken and there is nothing to tell you which century you are in.

Then comes winter, when hoar frost lingers under my garden hedge and foxes scream in the dead of night as if crucified by cold. In many ways this is the best time of all, a connoisseur's season of muted colours, when all Dorset becomes a watercolour wash of ghostly woods and bare horizons. The days may be short, but I revel in winter walks among the crooked oaks of Powerstock Common, and the teatime ritual of drawing the curtains to create a cave of warmth around the inglenook fire.

And even then, once Christmas has passed and the fieldfares have stolen the last hedgerow berries, there is the sure knowledge that already, down here in England's soft underbelly, spring is stirring as the first snowdrops emerge and the whole glorious cavalcade of the turning world is about to begin all over again.

A Carp Called Harry

South Dorset, September 1993

Carp fishermen are a curious breed: single-minded fanatics united by an obsession that drives sane men from their beds to sit all night on lonely vigils, waiting for the bite that never comes.

'Every true carp man carries the myth of the monster around in his head,' Chris Yates says, 'the dream of the big fish he hopes to catch one day.' Yates should know. In 1980 he landed a 51lb 8oz carp, the biggest freshwater fish ever caught in Britain. Now he and Bob James, his angling friend and greatest rival, are on the trail of an even bigger carp. And, having sworn to keep their destination secret, I have come to meet them.

This fish, thought to weigh at least seventy pounds, lives in a lake on a derelict country estate in the south of England, where Yates and James, both in their forties, have been hunting it for more than two years. 'We're trying to catch a fish that is twenty years older than me,' James says. 'We call her Harry – we didn't know she was female when we named her. She's a mirror carp and she has been swimming around in this lake since before World War II. She's a loner. And she is absolutely huge.'

The story of the monster fish first surfaced when Yates and James were working on *A Passion for Angling*, a six-part series screened by BBC2. During the filming, Yates and James met a gamekeeper who said he had seen a giant carp in a lake on the estate where he worked. It was, said the keeper, 'nearly four feet long and as thick across the back as my Labrador'. Once, he'd even heard it jumping out of the water. 'What did it sound like?' Yates asked him. 'Like a cow falling in,' replied the keeper.

The keeper's tale set Yates to thinking. He knew that Redmire Pool in Herefordshire, the most favoured carp water in Britain, had been stocked in the 1930s by a Surrey trout farmer called Donald Leaney. After Yates had caught his record carp at Redmire in 1980 the two men became friends, and when Leaney died in 1987 he left Yates his stock books. Yates searched through the books and found an entry dated January 1933, recording the release of two hundred four-inch carp in the secret lake. 'Now we knew the keeper's story was true,' Yates says.

Yates and James have identified about a dozen huge carp, all survivors from the original stock. So far, they have landed only one fish, a twenty-two-pound male, which Yates caught last year. As for Harry, they have seen her no more than half a dozen times in the last three years. 'On most carp lakes, carp show themselves by leaping,' James says. 'Here they never leap.'

The lost lake is just as Yates and James described it: seven acres of water covered with coots' nests, hemmed in by beech trees, with a chest-high jungle of burdock, nettles and willowherb on its banks. The water is clear, but nowhere can you see the bottom. Even now, somewhere down there, the big carp are lurking, dozing in the sunless deeps or rooting for bloodworms in the mud.

Carp are slow, amiable creatures, and as they grow old they become almost comatose. 'A monster like Harry probably stopped growing years ago,' James says. 'All she needs to do is keep on ticking over. That's why we see her so seldom.'

'Carp are blessed with acute vision,' Yates says. 'To be a carp fisherman you must never show yourself. You must melt into the background, become a tree, a sheep, anything but an angler.'

A photographer and successful writer of angling books, Yates has been a carp fisherman for thirty-five years. He is a true eccentric and an eternal traditionalist, scornful of new-fangled innovations, choosing instead to stalk his fish with a forty-year-old split-cane rod.

James, on the other hand, is the thoroughly modern carp man, equipped with the latest high-tech gizmos. His idea of fishing is to set his three carbon-fibre fishing rods on their triple-rod pod and go to sleep in his green canvas bivvy, safe in the knowledge that the bleep from his electronic bite-alarms will wake him if there's a fish around.

'Carp fishing is a waiting game,' he says. 'Using three rods shortens the odds. What I am doing is setting a trap and then backing off while the carp settle down and regain their equilibrium.'

A carp can sense everything. It knows the angler who is trying to catch it by the smell of his fingers on the bait. It will hide at the sound of a human voice. Of all freshwater fish, the carp is the shyest, the most cautious and the hardest to catch.

On this the two anglers are in agreement. Carp are cunning; 'salmon with brains', Yates calls them. 'There are one or two suckers that get caught at least once each season,' he says. 'But there are also some real whoppers that are never hooked. They change the rules. That's what makes fishing for them so exciting – the tension of the unpredictable.'

Carp are also fastidious feeders. In the old days, all kinds of ingenious and revolting baits were used. One called for raw bullocks' brains. Today, modern anglers like James use 'boilies' – marbles of soya and semolina paste – laced with chemical cocktails of amino acids, enzyme additives and a range of bizarre flavours, from fermented krill to peach melba.

'They stimulate the appetite,' James says. 'For a carp, it's the equivalent of walking past an Indian restaurant.' But as Yates points out, you can still catch them with a worm or a crust of bread. 'It's the angler who catches the fish,' he says. 'Not the bait.'

Until Yates landed his record carp at Redmire in 1980, the previous best had been a forty-four pounder called Clarissa, also caught at Redmire, by Dick Walker in 1952. After her capture, Clarissa was taken to the aquarium at London Zoo, where she lived for a further twenty-seven years.

'Dick Walker was the father of carp fishing in Britain,' Yates says. 'Until then, nobody dreamed that carp could grow so big. In those days, there were just a few regular carp fanatics. Now there are more than 150,000 – all willing to pay good money for the chance to catch a big one.'

Indeed, so popular has the sport become that it has given rise to a new breed of rural villain, the carp rustler. 'There's a flourishing black market in carp,' Yates says. 'People will pay two thousand pounds, no questions asked, for a really big fish.' The reason behind this skulduggery is not hard to fathom. Anyone owning a carp lake with a giant fish swimming around in it stands to make a tidy profit from increased angling fees.

'Hooking a big carp is like trying to stop a racehorse,' Yates says. 'It's a moment of pure vertigo. You feel the fish has caught you and is about to give you a severe beating for invading its domain. Euphoria and satisfaction come only when the fish is safely in the net.'

As for losing a big fish, this is the carp man's ultimate nightmare. 'When that happens,' Yates says, 'I've seen anglers hurl their tackle into the lake, bivouacs and all. I've even seen them throw fellow anglers in.'

The light fades. A dabchick draws a thin line across the lake's polished surface. The two carp hunters, ancient and modern, fish on as a tawny owl calls in the gathering dusk. In their minds and mine is the shared vision of a huge shadow rising from the weeds. Will it take the bait? If not, there is always solace in the carp man's motto: 'There's always tomorrow.'

Pebbles as Big as Skulls

Chesil Beach, Dorset, June 1998

Skylark numbers are declining in Britain, but you would never have guessed it at West Bexington. Here on the West Dorset coast the air over the National Trust fields was alive with them.

I was heading east towards Abbotsbury along the South West Coast Path, the longest walking trail in Britain, which runs west from Minehead in Somerset to Land's End and then doubles back along the Channel shore to Poole Harbour, a distance of 510 miles. Between me and the sea rose the Chesil Bank, a mighty ridge of wave-heaped shingle curling around Lyme Bay for eighteen miles, from West Bay harbour to Portland; and as I crunched along its pebbly margins I reminded myself that I was walking on one of the geological wonders of Europe. Its stones have been graded by the prevailing tides – from pea-sized gravel at West Bay to pebbles as big as skulls at Portland. In the old days, it was said, smugglers landing in the dead of night might judge where they were by the size of the stones on the beach.

In winter there is no shelter from the wild sou'-westerlies, and many a fine ship has come to grief on these inhospitable shores, having failed to beat its way to safety beyond the dinosaur snout of Portland Bill. During the great gale of 1824, two West Indiamen and a Danish brig were smashed to matchwood, and the government sloop *Ebenezer* was flung so high up on the beach that she was later hauled down on the other side and refloated on the brackish waters of the Fleet, Britain's biggest tidal lagoon, which extends all the way to Portland.

But today the Chesil Bank was in a more benign mood. Its tawny flanks shimmered in the heat haze of a perfect spring morning and the voice of the sea was hushed. As the year progressed, a few hardy wild flowers would emerge under the sea wind: thrift and campion, yellow-horned poppies and prickly clumps of ice-blue sea holly.

Ahead, the skyline rose with muscular symmetry to form the rounded brow of Abbotsbury Hill, and I could see the reed beds that mark the beginnings of the Fleet. It is here that the Chesil Bank assumes its full stature, rising in a forty-foot-high ridge between the Fleet and the sea.

Resist the temptation to bathe. The beach shelves steeply and is dogged by wicked undertows. Instead, follow the path that turns inland to Abbotsbury between green hills clearly imprinted with ancient field patterns. The building on the hilltop is the fourteenth-century Chapel of St Catherine, patron saint of spinsters, where lovelorn girls in former days would thrust a coin between its stones and offer up a prayer, whispering:

St Catherine, St Catherine, oh lend me thine aid
And grant that I niver may die an wold maid.
A husband, St Catherine,
A good one, St Catherine,
But arn-a-one better than narn-a-one, St Catherine.

Abbotsbury is a village of honey-coloured stone cottages and raised pavements, best visited out of season before its narrow main street becomes choked with traffic. Its Benedictine monastery was swept away by the Dissolution, but its monastic tithe barn, 270 feet long, survived, and is still thatched with reeds cut from the Fleet.

A short distance away and well worth a detour is Abbotsbury Swannery, established by the monks in the reign of the Plantagenet kings, where hundreds of mute swans breed every spring on their giant reed-cushion nests.

There is also a good pub in Abbotsbury – the Ilchester Arms – and from here I followed the old Bishops' Road out of the village to join the footpath up the grassy slopes of Abbotsbury Plains. Above me, a straggling row of wind-bent thorn bushes marked the line of the path as it toiled to the summit of White Hill. At the top I looked back, and there lay the village in its sleepy hollow, the chapel on its hill, the swans sailing on the Fleet and, beyond, the scythe-blade curve of the Chesil Bank outlined against the sea.

On White Hill I joined the alternative high-level route of the South West Coast Path that would take me all the way back to West Bexington. Designed to enable walkers to avoid Weymouth by cutting across country to Osmington Mills, it follows the prehistoric Dorset Coastal Ridgeway past the lonely barrows of Bronze Age warlords, and although the path lies a good mile inland you are never out of sight of the sea, which forms a glittering backdrop to some of the grandest panoramic views in the country.

Next morning, eager for a taste of the Chesil Bank's hinterland, I decided on a short foray into the Bride Valley, which lies between the coastal hills and the Dorset Downs. The Bride is a modest little river that rises near the village of Littlebredy and empties into the sea at Freshwater, near Burton Bradstock; but its lush and secretive countryside epitomises the deeply rural nature of West Dorset.

I followed a steep stony track out of West Bexington (signposted to Hardy's Monument), crossed the B3157 at Limekiln Hill and made for the Knoll, 590 feet above sea level. On top is a deserted stone building, a landmark visible for miles, once used as a shepherd's hut at lambing time. The climb will make you puff, but the reward is arguably the finest panorama of sea and countryside between here and Land's End.

Below I could see Cogden Beach – the western end of the Chesil Bank – and sunlight falling across the immense arc of Lyme Bay and the westering cliffs beyond, including the table-top silhouette of Golden Cap, the highest cliff on the English Channel. On a clear day you can see the Dartmoor tors and the South Devon coast running out to the pencil-thin outline of Start Point, forty miles away on the horizon.

From the Knoll I rejoined the metalled lane below and headed for Puncknowle (rhymes with funnel), with the Dorset Downs ahead on the northern skyline. I climbed a stile and dropped down a primrose lane into Puncknowle, a typical West Dorset village of stone and thatch set around a church with a twelfth-century Norman tower. Inside hangs a knightly helmet of the Napiers, who once lived in the mellow stone manor next door. Across the road is a pleasant small country pub, the Crown, selling Palmers beer from Bridport, the only brewery in Britain with a thatched roof.

From Puncknowle a path ran down through the cornfields to the trout pools and water meadows of the Bride Valley. There, beside a gnarled burr oak, I found a footbridge – built from a single massive slab of stone – and walked on through the fields to meet the road at Litton Cheney Youth Hostel.

Litton Cheney itself is a pleasant place to linger, watered by clear chalk streams that come bubbling out of the Downs, with waterside cottages reached by stone footbridges and gargoyles grimacing from its fifteenth-century church tower.

At the YHA I turned back to recross the Bride Valley by a different route, heading southeast across a little wooden bridge over the Bride, into a hidden world of cattle pastures and blackthorn hedges which has not changed since Hardy's day. I came to a country lane where yellowhammers wheezed from the telephone wires. I crossed a ford by an old stone house with swallows' nests under the eaves, and found myself in the middle of a farmyard. Had I taken a wrong turning? No – signposts steered me past Looke Farm (with the date 1700 carved in stone above the door), and on towards Tulk's Hill.

Now the path disappeared into a classic West Dorset 'gwyle', or gully, where badger trails wound through a mist of bluebells and a stream trickled down from Catholes Withy Bed. A steady climb over rumpled pastures took me past the woods of Green Leaze, where buzzards were wheeling overhead. From here I could see the familiar outline of the Knoll half a mile away; as I made my way towards it, the sea reappeared again to the south, and with it those incomparable views of the West Dorset coastline in all its Jurassic splendour.

The Farm that Time Forgot

Kingcombe, Dorset, July 1988

High summer, and the air over the meadow lies sultry, unstirred. Cloud castles are building in the midday haze and the horseflies are biting. Haymaking weather.

Making hay is essentially a midsummer affair. Traditionally the hay was cut on St John's Day (24 June), although there was never any need to consult the calendar. A farmer knew when the grass was ready for cutting simply by looking at the rich colours of the ripening seed-heads. But at Kingcombe, as in many parts of the Southwest, it had always been the custom to wait until July to allow the 'bottom grasses' to thicken up.

Swallows are scudding over the grass heads. Marbled white butterflies sun themselves on the knapweed flowers. Bees drone among the meadow thistles and grasshoppers give the heat a voice, drowsy and quivering like the air itself.

Such sights and sounds are much scarcer now. Old meadowland, that living tapestry draped so casually over so much of England, has been ripped away with scarcely a thought. In Somerset you can count the last old, true hay meadows on one hand. In Dorset the Nature Conservancy Council puts the loss of unimproved lowland meadows since 1949 at 95 per cent – the same as the average for the whole country. While we have been intent on protecting nature's rarities (otters, peregrines, bitterns, ospreys), someone has been stealing the grass from under our feet. Now only a few tattered fragments survive, and the best belong to Kingcombe.

Here in the valley of the little River Hooke, in the back of beyond to the west of Dorchester, is a nineteenth-century landscape of unshorn hedgerows and derelict meadows threaded by lanes that lead to nowhere. In many ways it is the epitome of Hardy's Wessex. And, for nearly seventy years, it was the centre of Arthur Walbridge's world.

The six-hundred-acre estate he bought in 1918 was never good agricultural land. It varied from undrained clay to acid greensand; but at least it was his.

The years slid by. World War II never touched Kingcombe. Nor, mercifully, did the agricultural revolution that was about to change the face of Britain. All round Kingcombe, while his neighbours were acquiring the machines and chemicals of modern farming, Arthur Walbridge and his sons stuck to the old ways, grazing their cattle and cutting their hay without recourse to herbicides and fertilisers.

No wonder the Nature Conservancy Council rushed to designate his land as a Site of Special Scientific Interest. Quite unintentionally, old Arthur Walbridge had created what has come to be called 'the farm that time forgot'. When he died in December 1985 there were fears that the land might fall into unsympathetic hands. Fortunately most of it was saved for the nation by the Dorset Wildlife Trust, which is now working to maintain its extraordinary diversity of grassland species.

These old hay meadows belonged to a way of life that allowed nature and humankind to co-exist. In the old days, before the advent of artificial fertilisers, grass grew in its own sweet way, enriched by nothing more radical than the cowpat. It was cut in summer; then the cattle were turned out to graze on the aftermath.

Such a meadow might contain a hundred or more flowering plants and a dozen different grasses, including the sweet vernal grass whose plumed panicles hold the essence of summer – a natural oil called coumarin that gives old meadows their new-mown fragrance.

Over the centuries a gentle equilibrium had been reached, but the twentieth century blundered down a different path, more productive, but at a heavy cost. Our modern fields, sown with a few surrogate strains, are a poor substitute for the miraculous life-support system they have supplanted. Of the 117 wildflowers considered most seriously at risk in Britain, thirty-four belong to the grasslands. And, while natural grassland may support twenty species of butterflies, artificial improved grassland supports none.

In the nineteenth century Richard Jefferies could write about the corncrakes that skulked in the hay meadows of southern England. Their rasping cries, like running a finger down the teeth of a comb, were as familiar as the cuckoo. Now modern farming has banished them to the remotest Scottish islands.

Not even Kingcombe can boast a corncrake; only finches and skylarks, and an occasional sparrowhawk hunting along the woodland edges. In fact there is nothing nationally rare at all except the grassland communities themselves. The beauty of the place is its simplicity. It is the kind of countryside we once took for granted, filled with a litany of yesterday's flowers: cowslips and spotted orchids, yellow rattle, meadow vetchling.

In the Middle Ages these Kingcombe meadowlands were divided by wooden stakes into long strips called doles that reverted to common grazing once the hay had been cut. The parish map of 1868 still shows these divisions, together with their old field names: Yonder Cowleaze, Neals Mead, Mowlands Common.

Today the names are almost forgotten, like those of the labourers who swung the scythes and forked the hay; but the boundaries of the medieval doles are still there for all to see, no longer staked but fossilised for posterity by banks and hedgerows whose presence adds to Kingcombe's sense of continuity. To keep this complex mosaic going, the traditional regime of mowing and grazing must be continued; and this month the old farm will yield its first proper harvest for the new owners.

Meanwhile, out in the fields the grass stands tall, thigh-deep if you were to wade through it, stirring up butterflies at every step. From a distance it had looked more brown than green, tawny as a lion's flank; but close up it dissolves into myriad shades of mauve and tan and olive seed-heads, shot through with the glitter of buttercups, rust-red sorrel, the deeper green of ribwort plantain, and white drifts of oxeye daisies. It looks like being a bumper crop.

Waiting for a Bite

River Stour, Dorset, December 1988

The instructions were explicit. 'Go through muddy gate and across field. Please keep at least five yards from the river bank and approach my fishing spot at a crouching stalk.' My friend Hugh Miles had promised to introduce me to the arcane world of the roach fisherman.

As one of the world's top wildlife film cameramen Miles has the perfect temperament for roach fishing. His patience is endless, his optimism impervious to rain and cold. When I found him he had already been fishing the Dorset Stour since dawn.

December is a favourite month for roach. In May, when the river is loud with the harsh song of sedge warblers, the fish move upstream to spawn, but return with the autumn spates to settle down for winter in deeper water.

The Stour is a classic roach river, deep and slow. The stretch where Miles was fishing, in the water meadows between Belcher's Hole and Corfe Mullen, belongs to the Southampton Piscatorial Society. In 1987 it produced three monster roach of more than three pounds – one of them caught by Miles himself last Christmas Eve.

Three pounds may not sound like a big fish unless you know that the average roach weighs under a pound. For most anglers a two-pound roach is the fish of a lifetime, and a three-pounder is the stuff that anglers' dreams are made of. Catch one of these leviathans and fame is assured. You will go into the record books alongside the great roach hunters of the past: men like Wilfred Cutting of Hornsea Mere in Yorkshire, and present-day heroes such as Owen Wentworth and Gerry Swanton.

Young roach are shoal fish, seeking safety in numbers; but big roach are loners. Like old bull elephants they leave the herd to end their days in solitary. Veterans of the river, they have learned to avoid the pike's fierce rush, the tempting titbits that hide barbed hooks. They are not lusty or tenacious fighters, but they are old and wise. Their numbers are few and their caution is legendary – hence the obsession of the truly dedicated roach men and their cold winter vigils, waiting for the bite that seldom comes.

Today the conditions are not promising. Not enough colour in the river, rain in the air and a blustery wind sending flurries of wild cats' paws across the water.

Wellies sinking in the bankside ooze, I join Miles under his fisherman's umbrella and squat on a campstool as he explains the technique of 'long-trotting'. This is the art of presenting a naturally moving bait – and one that also enables the angler to cover every inch of the swim where a fish may be lying.

The best spot to fish is the crease – the borderline between the slack water where roach like to rest and the faster current where they feed. The skill lies in guiding the float, letting it drift with the river so that the bait is offered head-on. A clumsy presentation is fatal and will only scare the fish away. But first the river must be explored with a plummet to gauge the correct depth at which to find the bottom-dwelling roach. Miles also takes a thermometer to test the water – roach won't feed below forty-two degrees Fahrenheit. Today it registers fifty-four degrees – lukewarm for December.

Next, the ground bait, traditionally one of the coarse fisherman's most powerful weapons. In the old days all kinds of ingenious and revolting recipes were used. Some called for human fat and powdered skulls. But Miles is content to use stale bread and ground hemp seed. He knows the roach is a hemp seed junkie.

The tools of his trade are a fourteen-foot carbon-fibre rod; a centre-pin reel handmade in Ringwood; a size twelve fine wire hook with a wicked little chemically sharpened barb; modern, pre-stretched monofilament nylon line with two-and-a-half-pound breaking strain; and a bird-quill float with a bright orange tip and balsawood body sensitive enough to dip at the nudge of an inquisitive minnow.

Now the long wait begins, relieved only by occasional swigs from Miles' hip flask – a warming mixture of whisky and Drambuie that keeps the cold at bay. Once settled, the dedicated roach man won't even shuffle his feet for fear that the canny fish will pick up the vibrations. If disturbed, they will retreat into the weed or sulk under the bank for the rest of the day.

The rod flicks out, the float drifts down, a solitary orange spark among the grey ripples. Somewhere down there the roach will be hovering, suspended in the Stour's green gloom. In my mind's eye I can see him, a beautiful fish, humpbacked and deep-bellied with flame-red fins and silver chain-mail flanks. I imagine the bait, a mere flake of bread pinched on to the hook, and the fish eyeing it warily before inching forward; the small toothless mouth opening to suck at the morsel like a fastidious old dowager toying with a canapé.

Suddenly the float goes down. A bite; a strike; Miles reels in, but it is only a minnow, a bright fingerling – the staple diet of pike, perch and kingfishers. Two years old and fully grown, it will spawn in the spring and then die, its brief life spent.

It would be exciting to tell you that at the end of the day Miles caught his roach. It would also be untrue. Roach fishing is not like that. Sometimes, towards dusk, roach will rise to the surface and then roll under – a sign that the fish are about to feed – but not today. The gentle giants of the Stour have beaten us.

We stay on until the lights of Corfe Mullen begin to glimmer across the melancholy fields and it is too dark to see the float. By now I know I'll never make a roach man. I lack the stoicism that enables the true fisherman to endure hour after patient hour sitting bunched with cramped limbs in the flesh-pinching chill of a December afternoon. Worse still, I do not possess the angler's single-mindedness, being too easily distracted by the life of the river. A trio of mute swans float past like icebergs in the swirling current, and my mind drifts with them.

I may not be a fisherman, but at least I share the angler's love of the river and its restfulness, the emptiness and silence of the midwinter landscape. Bournemouth's busy streets are only ten miles away, but out here in the wind and rain England is still wild, elemental, unchanging.

The Leys of the Land

Eggardon Hill, Dorset, January 1974

The wind blew icy cold. Tracers of sleet raked my anorak with each passing gust. Caught in the crossfire with nowhere to hide I slogged on up the scarp, knee joints cracking like bonfire twigs.

I was heading for the Belstone. No Alpine pinnacle, this; merely a modest limestone ledge capping the final westernmost flourish of the Wessex Downs. Below the sweep of plummeting turf, trod by generations of sheep into a Liverpool Kop of grassy terraces, the landscape spreads out like a map. From this buzzard's-eye viewpoint on the Belstone Ledge, eight hundred feet above the knolls and combes of the greensand country, you can see Dartmoor on a clear day.

What had dragged me from my hearthside into the raw January daylight was not the view, incomparable though it is, but a book, *The Old Straight Track*, by Alfred Watkins. It was first published in 1925 but I must confess I stumbled across it only last month. Watkins, a keen amateur archaeologist, noticed in his native Herefordshire how conspicuous landmarks such as beacon hills, knolls, mounds, moats, standing stones, prehistoric barrows and old churches built on pre-Christian sites frequently seemed to fall into straight lines. Further field research led him to the revolutionary conclusion that not only Herefordshire but the whole of Britain was crisscrossed in this manner, the landmarks serving as signposts for an invisible network of long-lost trackways laid down centuries before the Romans superimposed their own legionary trunk-route system.

Watkins called these old straight tracks 'leys', claiming that they were aligned and marked out by an elitist class of Celtic astronomer-shamans, revered for their ancient powers. According to Watkins, these ley-men must have had class names applied to them, just as the Smiths of the world have inherited their surname from the profession of blacksmith. The Watkins theory, based on the frequency with which the names 'Dod', 'Black' and 'Cole' (or 'Cold') occur along ley lines, is that there were once a Dodman, Blackman and Coleman, prehistoric surveyors setting their sightlines across the untrammelled landscapes of pagan Britain.

Some ley lines follow proven Midsummer Day sunrise alignments. A classic sun-ley runs down from Inkpen Beacon through Stonehenge and Cerne Abbas, where the turf-cut figure of the Cerne Giant, Britain's first full-frontal nude, flaunts his virility on the Dorset Downs, to end above Chesil Beach at Puncknowle Beacon.

More intriguing still is the thought that the entire network of alignments, when locked together, forms a grand design that may have had some deeper, more religious significance. Certainly many of the most prominent landmarks are beacon hills, where until quite recent times bale fires were lit in homage to Baal, the Babylonian sun god who became part of the Celtic pantheon.

So there I stood on the Belstone Ledge to test the Watkins theory. Slowly the smoking sky cleared. The sun lit the land and suddenly knolls, mounds, church towers, clumps of Scots pines and all the humpy hills of Wessex leapt into focus around me. Sadly, amateur Dodman that I am, I could get none of them to align. But strolling back down the ridge above the common I stopped to stand upon a solitary tumulus that commands the skyline, and a strange thing happened.

Across the fields I could clearly see Toller Porcorum church tower; and behind it, peeping over the Downs like a periscope, was the flagstaff of Cattistock church tower in exact alignment with that of Toller.

Back home I plotted my newfound ley line on the local Ordnance Survey map and discovered that it ran from the Neolithic hill fort on Hambledon Hill by way of Up Cerne church, Cattistock and Toller to the tumulus on the common. From there it led directly through the earthworks of Athelstan's castle mound to Loders church and St Andrew's Well, ending at another tumulus five hundred feet above the coast on Thorncombe Beacon.

From the same map I produced a number of other possible sightlines. The best one began at West Bay harbour and headed through the same St Andrew's Well (five leys appear to intersect here) to Bradpole church, Mangerton Hill, Hackthorn Hill, the Hoar Stones on Toller Down, Corscombe church, a moated farm, a Roman site, Halstock church, Sutton Bingham church, Barwick church, Marston Magna church, and then off the map to Castle Cary and who knows what final destination.

Coincidence? Watkins also had his doubts, but made this experiment: he took a map sheet of the Andover area containing fifty-one churches. In eight separate instances he found that four churches fell on a straight line and in one instance he found a five-church alignment. Watkins then took a similar-sized sheet of paper and marked fifty-one random crosses on it. When he tried to align these he was able to find only one instance of four points falling into line, and none of five.

Make of it what you will. Maybe there is a mystery to be revealed if we could only read the language of the leys. I have since spent hours trying to pinpoint mounds, mark-trees, crossways and standing stones. Look to your own maps and try it in your own area. How many tumps, touts, church towers or beacon hills can you line up?

If nothing else, it certainly makes map reading more fun.

Staying Ahead of the Pack

Nettlecombe, Dorset, December 1984

Boxing Day, and the going is soft underfoot. There is no wind to disperse the quick, sharp taint of fox in the lane; a grand day for the hunt, but a bad one for the hunted. The ash on the hill is black with rooks. They stare expectantly from the bare branches like an undertakers' convention waiting for a corpse to bury.

For the first time I hear the horn, faint and far off. From the crest of the knoll I look for movement in the rolling spread of fields below. There they are: a distant glimpse of brindled hounds, plunging like porpoises in a sea of kale, and a whipper-in, one solitary scarlet spark against a sombre coppice.

Suddenly there is a crash of sound and the baying of hounds grows deeper, more menacing. Hidden by the hill, the music comes closer. I wait in the hedge for the entry of the fugitive. He appears within minutes, a big dog fox going flat out across the ploughland, his winter coat the colour of dead bracken, his long tail fluffed out behind. He doesn't run; he flows through the furrows, three fields ahead of the pack.

Flying in his wake come the hounds, crying on a sure line as they burst through the first hedge in a tan and cream chevron. As yet there is no sign of the huntsmen, but already the fox's lead is cut to two fields and shrinking fast as he drops into Combe Bottom. Then follows confusion: milling hounds, stampeding sheep, startled rooks swirling overhead. The hunt is foxed.

How has it happened? Maybe it is wrong to read cunning into animal behaviour. To suggest that the fox had deliberately planned this diversion would be to credit him with powers he cannot possess. But his tactics are faultless. A quick twist and he is doubling back up the combe while the pack is still casting around to pick up his line again as the first riders arrive, red-faced and breathless on mud-spattered horses.

By now other onlookers have gathered. Nearby stands a father with three sons. We are the only ones to have seen the fox reappear. 'You won't tell, will you?' said one of the boys anxiously. Together we watch the fox race through a cottage garden among rows of sprout stalks stripped for Christmas, into a farmyard where his scent would be smothered by richer smells, and away to the sanctuary of Knoll Wood.

Why does foxhunting cause such bitter controversy? Is it really just a question of blood and cruelty on the one side, sport and tradition on the other? Or do the old antagonisms go deeper? There are those who would argue that the hunt is a ritual: a reaffirmation of the power of the gentry, a rubbing of Norman salt into Saxon wounds that nine hundred years of history have failed to heal.

My own views are hopelessly ambivalent. To watch a hunt streaming across a watercolour landscape of stubble, combe and spinney is to know the quintessence of the countryside in winter: all England distilled into one classic sporting print. I accept, too, that some foxes must be culled; that in the absence of other predators a balance must be achieved. Yet I cannot deny the relief I felt when I watched that fox go free.

A Forest Fit for Merlin

Powerstock, Dorset, December 1984

It is always now, in the hungover aftermath of the Christmas holiday, that winter seems to bite harder. Hoar frost lingers all day under the hedges and the ground is iron underfoot. But it was not the cold that urged us over the fields at a forced-march tempo. Our walk had the purpose and precision of a military exercise. Fuel for free was our objective: the need to top up our dwindling log stack with dead wood.

Today we were off to the wood where the fallow deer live. There I knew the pickings would be easy. The forest floor is a charnel house of dead limbs shaken loose from geriatric oaks by the gales that come blustering up the valley from Lyme Bay. A modest-sized power station could no doubt consume the entire wood in a week, but there is more than enough to keep us going.

No ordinary wood, this. Wild and wolfish in the winter light, it pours across the head of the combe in a writhing tide of tangled boughs, dank and lichen-bearded. It is of the same wizened pedigree as Wistman's Wood on Dartmoor; and its goblin oaks exude the same vague air of disquiet. Why should the silence under those misshapen candelabras appear so sinister? It is a forest fey enough for Merlin. Above looms the dark presence of Eggardon, where motorists coming by night over the Roman road are still afraid to look in the rear-view mirror lest they glimpse the ghost of a woman who has been known to appear, unbidden, in the back seat.

The wood is a remnant, a relic of the primeval oak wood that once covered most of Britain. It was here in King Athelstan's reign, before the Norman Conquest. (There is still a King's Farm on the edge of the forest.) It was here long before the Romans trod their road over the downs from Dorchester. It is as old as the Stone Age, one of those rare and diminishing scraps of the land surface where humankind has made little impact.

Ours has been an age of unprecedented woodland destruction. All over Britain, from Dorset to the Highlands, the woods are falling fast. In the past thirty years we have lost half our ancient semi-natural woodlands, and still the devastation continues. But what are ancient woodlands, and why should we preserve them? The Nature Conservancy Council's definition is a site that has been wooded since at least 1600. Some of these old woods may have originated in the Dark Ages, and studies by historical ecologists such as Dr Oliver Rackham show that some are older still. They may well be direct descendants of what he called the wildwood – the primeval forest that covered Britain after the last Ice Age.

Today Britain, after Ireland, is the most naked country in Europe. The old wildwood is gone forever, but what remains is even more precious: a scattered mosaic of clumps and coppices, silent spinneys, lonely fox roosts, Hampshire beech hangers, Wealden shaws, pagan groves of oak and holly; and sometimes, among the bare trunks, the dark shadows receding, the echo of a true forest.

Such was the wood we entered today. The frost had not penetrated its boggy bottoms, and the ground squelched underfoot, threatening to suck the boots from our feet. Winding between tall clumps of pendulous sedge, we left a trail of muddy footprints, each one slowly filling with water. Nor were ours the only tracks. Incised in black humus and yellow clay were the cloven slots of fallow deer, for which the wood is a refuge from poachers.

When the light began to fail we retraced our steps. In the wood's hollow heart, with no landmarks to steer by, it is all too easy to lose one's way. Dusk seeped like silt between the trees. The toadstool smell of rotting wood and leaf mould hung in the air, thick as Monday's washing. Somewhere a robin sang a requiem for the dying day. Twice we were brought up sharp by a rope of scent stretched taut across the track – the rancid reek of fox.

Back home the gathered branches were snapped into burnable lengths and packed into the log basket. Outside in the dark the frost was fierce. Was that why the vixen up on the hill screamed with such anguish? The curtains were drawn against the night. The room had become a cave of warmth, flickering in the firelight's glow. Wet from the wood, the logs hissed in the flames. The teapot stood by the fire. The hearth gods were happy and so was I. Lopez the tabby came in from the kitchen to curl up on the rug, and together we warmed ourselves in the released energy of ancient sunlight stored up in summers long ago when the oaks were young.

SOUTH

To return to the downs. Their very emptiness and desolation, which frightens the stranger from them, only serves to make them more fascinating to those who are intimate with and have learned to love them. It may be fancy, or the effect of contrast, but it has always seemed to me that just as the air is purer and fresher on these chalk heights than on the earth below, and as the water is of a more crystal purity, and the sky perhaps bluer, so do all colours and all sounds have a purity and vividness and intensity beyond that of other places.

from A Shepherd's Life *by W. H. Hudson*

Looking for Laurie under a
Cotswold Sky

Slad, Gloucestershire, April 2014

*'That was the day we came to the village, in the summer of the last year
of the First World War. To a cottage that stood in a half-acre of garden
on a steep bank above a lake… and all for three and sixpence a week.'*

In the Gloucestershire village of Slad, near Stroud, the cottage still
stands above the lake, but the man who grew up there and wrote
those words now lies in the churchyard across the road beneath a
simple stone engraved with a spray of wild roses.

Laurie Lee died in May 1997 at the age of eighty-two, but *Cider
with Rosie*, the lyrical portrait of his Cotswold boyhood, has become
an enduring classic in which, more than any other writer since Hardy,
he captured the essence of a special corner of England and made it
his own.

On the roof of Gloucestershire the long flat fields stretch away
under the sky, a sporting-print landscape dotted with lonely fox
coverts and cross-stitched with more than four thousand miles of
low drystone walls. But very different is the countryside Laurie
Lee immortalised, in the southern Cotswolds around Stroud and
Painswick, where the high roads suddenly take leave of their senses
and plunge suicidally into a wooded tangle of deep-set valleys with
the village of Slad at its epicentre.

Don't expect to find the picture-book beauty of the classic Cotswold tourist honeypots with their trout streams and gastro pubs. 'It never was a show village,' Lee once said of the place he called home.

The original road through the village lies below the newer one along which traffic now hurtles from Stroud towards Birdlip and which Lee, who never learned to drive, hated with a passion. When he was a child the only car in Slad belonged to the Squire, and even today there are no streetlights to pollute the Cotswolds' star-spangled night skies.

By the roadside lies the same steep bank on which the young Laurie was set down at the age of three, lost in a forest of June grasses taller than himself, until his sisters came to scoop him up and take him into the house that would be home for the next sixteen years. Now called Rosebank, it is still there and has since become a listed building, moss-flaked tiles, corrugated lean-to kitchen, half-acre garden and all. Originally a modest seventeenth-century manor, it had long since decayed by the time Lee's family arrived and was split into three separate dwellings, the other two occupied by two ancient grannies – ''Er-Up-Top' and ''Er-Down-Under'.

Here he lived with Annie, his mother, and his seven siblings, wolfing down suppers of lentil stew, reading by lamplight, building a bookcase from a discarded rabbit hutch that he nailed to his bedroom wall and filled with the works of Dickens, Yeats and D. H. Lawrence. And outside and all around lay the valley itself, complete and beautiful, a natural playground of buttercup fields and bramble jungles, packhorse tracks and badger setts in which he and his feral friends – sly Arnold, Spadge Hopkins, Walt Kerry and the rest – ran wild, playing Fox and Hounds in the moonlit woods and yelling, 'Whistle-or-'OLLER! Or-we-shall-not-FOLLER!'

As for the eponymous Rosie, in whose arms he famously lay entwined under a wagon at haymaking time, she was 'just a composite', said Lee when pressed, a portrait drawn from half a dozen girls he had known.

In an age without regular newspapers, radio or TV, the village he described existed in a bubble of self-sufficiency, cut off from the outside world by the wooded crests of its enfolding hills. Lee was growing up in the sunset of a rural England in which the old order, shaken to its roots by the Great War, would never be the same again.

When he was born, the horse was king and life still moved, as Laurie put it, 'at the same pace as Caesar's', until the first brass-lamped motor cars with their solid rubber tyres came spluttering up the valley, putting an end to a thousand years of silence.

Cider with Rosie is more than autobiography. It is Lee's thanksgiving for those early years, freeze-framing a moment in time and thus preserving it for ever in his bittersweet prose, not only the valley's bucolic countryside with its dusty roads that smelt of cow dung, but also its accompanying hardship, poverty and brutish violence.

Although clearly a labour of love, the book took two years to complete and was rewritten three times. Published in 1959, it sold more than six million copies and has never been out of print.

Kathy Lee, Laurie's widow, still lives in the eighteenth-century cottage they bought in Slad with the proceeds of *Cider With Rosie*, and I met her quite by chance on my first day in the area. I was lunching in Nailsworth and a waitress introduced me to her. Now in her eighties, her cornflower-blue eyes are still as clear as when they beguiled Laurie, and sparkled mischievously when she described their first date together – an evening at the cinema when he was thirty-two and she not yet fifteen. They married in London three years later.

Their cottage lies just below the Woolpack, the village pub whose name is a reminder of the days when cloth mills thrived in the valley. Inside, in an end room smelling of wood smoke, is where Laurie held sway in his regular corner by the back window, from which he could lean out and take calls from home on his cordless phone and conduct business while enjoying a pint.

In the Woolpack I met Adam Horovitz, a Slad Valley poet and long-time friend of Laurie Lee who volunteered to show me around. 'I can see him now in his fedora and white suit,' he said, 'half gentleman, half roguish Gloucestershire boy.'

Across the road stands the single-storey schoolhouse in which its most famous pupil and his fellow classmates sat side by side at wooden desks with china inkwells, chanting, 'Twice-two-are-four, One-George-is-King' as the sun slanted in through its mullion windows.

From there we strolled down the lane past the Squire's house with its Georgian façade, where Laurie and his friends would go carol-singing with candles in jam jars to light their way, and came to the valley bottom where the tragic Miss Flynn, a pale pre-Raphaelite beauty, threw off her clothes and was found floating face up in the opaque waters of Jones's Pond.

'Can you believe it?' said Horovitz, gesturing towards the top end of the valley. 'There used to be a brothel up there in the heyday of the cloth mills.'

It would be foolish to imagine that the countryside around Slad has not changed, or that rural life was better in Lee's young days. Stroud has expanded. Roads are busier. Noise, pollution and insensitive development have all conspired to diminish its spell. Slad Valley lies within the Cotswold Area of Outstanding Natural Beauty, but that has not prevented property speculators from trying to lay their hands on it. Sometimes it seems as if only the ghost of Laurie Lee himself has held them at bay, and there is still talk of plans to build a hundred or more houses at the foot of the valley. 'Laurie would have been horrified,' said Kathy.

Yet in spite of everything the magic endures, in the tilted fields where you can still lie in the grass and let the summer wash over you, among the orchids, fox earths and banks of wild garlic, and in the blue twilight rolling down the valley from Sheepscombe, where the woods Lee's Uncle Charlie planted on thirty-five shillings a week are now mature cathedrals of mighty beech boles.

It belongs to a part of England that still moves to the slow swing of the seasons, from winter frosts to harvest time, where the villages that rooted themselves centuries ago on the sloping hillsides have clung on in spite of change, wrapped in a gentle sadness as if in mourning for a bygone countryside that everyone believed might last for ever.

In Search of King Alfred

Berkshire Ridgeway, January 1988

The Ridgeway is the oldest road in Britain. To follow it over the Berkshire Downs from Streatley to Avebury, some forty miles away in Wiltshire, is to tread a path trampled into the landscape by five thousand years of travellers. Roman legions, Iron Age warriors, the Ridgeway has known them all. But seldom can it have seen a more formidable army than the one that passed this way eleven centuries ago.

The year was 871, when England was not yet a nation and Aethelred was king of the West Saxons, whose lands extended over Berkshire, Wiltshire, Hampshire, Dorset and Somerset. In January an invading Danish army moved from its base at Reading and struck deep into Aethelred's kingdom, marching west along the Ridgeway. Ahead of them the Saxons lay in wait at the foot of the Downs; and it was there, while the king was at prayers, that Alfred, his younger brother, spotted the enemy and led his men to victory.

The Battle of Ashdown, as it became known, heralded one of the most crucial periods in England's history and introduced Alfred as the man who became the founding father of the English nation.

Alfred was not only a redoubtable warrior king, he was also a Latin scholar, a lawmaker and an educator, who formed the government and founded the Royal Navy. Yet for all his achievements he remains an elusive, almost mythical figure, and one day in autumn, on an impulse, I set out to trace Alfred's footsteps across his former kingdom.

My journey began in Britain's oldest public museum, the Ashmolean, in Oxford. Among its treasures one shines out brighter than the rest: a gold jewel dug up in a field near Athelney in Somerset in 1693. To prove its pedigree it bears an Anglo-Saxon inscription: *Aelfred mec heht gewyrcan* (Alfred had me made). I stared at it and the centuries fell away. Here was an object that had been held in the king's own hand, a tangible link with the visionary leader who saved his country from the fury of the Vikings.

From Oxford I drove south across the Vale of the White Horse to Wantage, where Alfred was born in 849. A statue of him stands in the market square, and I asked a stallholder what he knew about the town's most famous son. 'There's an old pub around the corner where I believe he used to drink,' the man replied without a trace of irony.

Ahead rose the Downs, the high, bare chalklands, rolling away to Wiltshire. Somewhere up there was fought the Battle of Ashdown. The exact site is unknown, although local tradition places it near the Uffington White Horse.

This mysterious, stylised figure, more dragon than horse, is the oldest of about seventeen white horses etched into the downland turf of southern England. Most are nothing but eighteenth- and nineteenth-century graffiti carved by local squires and landowners. But the Uffington Horse has flowed along the rim of the Downs for two thousand years.

It is best seen from the road below. Close up, it is hard to make head or tail of it. All you see is a series of chalk trenches, 360 feet long. Below the horse is a flat-topped knoll where local legend says St George slew the dragon; and on the skyline stands Uffington Castle, an Iron Age hill fort with grassy ramparts and far-reaching views across the Vale.

Alfred was only twenty-one when he fought at Ashdown. That same year he became king, only to be trounced by the Danes in his next battle. For the next four years they tightened their hold over England until, in 876, under Guthrum, their leader, they decided to crush Alfred once and for all.

The king was celebrating Christmas at Chippenham, in Wiltshire, when Guthrum struck. On Twelfth Night the Danes came south, like wolves through the snow, to seize Chippenham and put Alfred to flight. He became a fugitive, hiding out in Athelney, deep in the Somerset marshes, and there, his kingdom reduced to a few square miles of impenetrable reed beds, he lived like an outlaw until the spring of 878, when he raised a fresh army and marched over Salisbury Plain to destroy Guthrum's army at the Battle of Edington. Guthrum himself was captured and baptised in Alfred's presence at Aller, in Somerset.

There is still a village called Edington, near Westbury, and on the Downs above is an Iron Age fort. Today it is a peaceful spot where people fly kites and walk their dogs among the prehistoric ramparts. But this could have been the site of Alfred's greatest victory, when England's future was decided in savage hand-to-hand combat.

It is hard to imagine how England must have looked in those days, when wolves still roamed the trackless woods and half of Somerset was an undrained fen. But sometimes, in the quiet fields between the power lines and the motorways, you stumble on a secret tract of country where it takes no great leap of imagination to conjure up the vanished face of Dark Age Wessex.

The Somerset Levels are such a place. Coming from the south, the green hills of Dorset sink into a waterlogged flatness of willows and cattle pastures mapped with the grey gleam of dykes. In its midst lies Muchelney, whose Saxon name means big island. Sometimes in winter, when the floods are up, Muchelney and its abbey ruins become an island again, marooned as it was in Alfred's day.

In the village of Aller, not far away, a signpost steered me to a boggy fourteenth-century church surrounded by boggy fields. No trace of Alfred's original church remains; but this was where Guthrum was baptised after his defeat at Edington. In the churchyard a robin sang. Beyond the trees, sleek cattle grazed. Time had moved on a thousand years, but it was still possible to imagine that solemn moment of English history being enacted here.

On the road to Burrow Bridge a sign nailed to a gatepost by some unsteady hand advertised local scrumpy. Somerset is cider country, and in every village orchard windfall apples lay in the long grass. At Burrow Bridge, in the shadow of the strange pyramidal hill called Burrow Mump, there is a pub called the King Alfred. I sensed I was getting close to the king's guerrilla stronghold, and another mile further on I found it.

Here was Athelney, a modest mound no more than thirty feet high, which had once hidden England's saviour in a sea of reeds. Today, nothing but an obelisk marks the spot, but you can still drive along the causeway the king's men built.

Often, when following Alfred's trail, it was easy to be thrown off the scent by other attractions. Which is why, returning through

Wiltshire, I found myself sidetracked by Silbury Hill, the enigmatic prehistoric mound that stands beside the A4 near Avebury. Experts reckon it must have taken eighteen million man-hours to build, but no one knows what it was for.

As for Avebury itself, of all ancient sites in these islands it is among the most impressive. You come upon it suddenly and, almost before you realise, you are inside its encircling banks and ditches, surrounded by standing sarsen stones twice the height of a man. And then the final surprise of finding an entire village – pub, cottages, church and manor – locked within its pagan rings.

Although our prehistoric ancestors chose to live on the Downs, it was the chalkland valleys with their pure springs and trout streams that drew later settlers. Here, in medieval times, arose the villages one sees today, with their cottages of mellow brick or creamy local Chilmark stone, their thatched pubs, mill houses and Norman churches. The rivers of these gentle valleys – Test, Itchen, Avon, Wylie – are revered by anglers and in early summer when the willows preside over seas of buttercups there is nowhere so quintessentially English.

And so to Winchester to seek out Alfred's last resting place. His statue, erected in 1901, stands in the Broadway, sword aloft, guarding the city that was once his capital. Even today, when exploring Winchester's medieval core, you follow the street plan he laid down. Winchester's cathedral is filled with the bones of Saxon kings, including those of Aethelwulf, Alfred's father. But where was Alfred himself? I had felt sure I would find him here, but he remained elusive to the end.

When he died, aged fifty, in 899, said a woman at Winchester Museum, he was buried in the Saxon Minster, whose foundations had been exposed outside the present cathedral's west door. But his remains were moved long ago.

Eventually, in King Alfred's Place, a suburban back street just outside the city walls, I found the ruined gateway of what was once the medieval Hyde Abbey. 'Burial place of Alfred the Great, his queen and their son, Edward the Elder' said a plaque on the wall. I read it and the words of G. K. Chesterton's poem, *The Ballad of the White Horse*, ran through my mind.

> *A sea-folk blinder than the sea*
> *Broke all about his land,*
> *But Alfred up against them bare*
> *And gripped the ground and grasped the air,*
> *Staggered and strove to stand.*

Between the Woods and the Water

New Forest, Hampshire, March 1997

Even in early spring, the A337 between Brockenhurst and Lyndhurst was echoing to a constant stream of traffic. But half a mile from the road, opposite the Balmer Lawn Hotel, I climbed a stile and followed the beery brown Lymington River into an older, quieter world.

Hampshire's New Forest is the last great wild space in England's soft underbelly. Within its 150 square miles – an area roughly the size of the Isle of Wight – is a landscape of heaths, mires and ancient woodlands without equal in Western Europe; a living medieval manuscript handed down from the days of the Norman kings.

Within five minutes of leaving the road a sudden movement caught my eye. From beyond an aisle of great oaks, three fallow deer were watching me: two bucks with sweeping antlers and a smaller doe. For a moment they lingered, then turned and bounded silently away, mere shadows melting into a gloom of holly.

Many an ancestral park is graced by herds of fallow deer, but these are truly wild. They have lived here longer than anyone can remember – perhaps since Roman times. They were certainly here when William the Conqueror created the New Forest in 1073 as his exclusive hunting ground, an easy day's ride from his royal capital in Winchester. In 1851 a Deer Removal Act was passed to encourage the growth of more timber, but the animals proved too canny to eradicate. Today six hundred fallow deer roam the forest, competing for browsing with smaller numbers of roe, sika and red deer, commoners' cattle and New Forest ponies.

Not all fallow deer have the dappled chestnut coats of the ornamental parkland herds. In colour they range from donkey brown to almost black, and white animals are not uncommon. They also differ in size from the ornamental herds, because here there are no fat fields to feed in. Instead, they must forage in the forest, and are therefore altogether leaner and lighter, although the bucks still produce good heads.

In autumn, caught up in the throes of the rut, the bucks compete with each other for the right to mate. At this time of year their necks are swollen with lust as they lay down their challenge, an eerie, rhythmic, rattling grunt, like a motorbike being kick-started into life. To listen to them in the falling dusk is to hear a sound as old as England itself, an echo from the Saxon wildwood that stood here long before the Conqueror made the New Forest his own.

The fawns are born in June. Only male deer carry antlers and it takes a full year for the first ones to appear: twin stubby spikes sheathed in velvet until August. In its second summer the young male with his six-inch antlers is called a pricket. The second head is shed in spring, and within weeks a new growth develops, bigger than the last, with brow and trey tines. Now, in the language of the forest, he is a sorel; and when the antlers produce the typical broad-bladed ends with finger-like tips known as spellers he becomes a bare buck. At the age of seven the head will be at its most magnificent, and although he may see several more winters the antlers will regress and never be so fine again.

Like the deer, the forest was still wrapped in the colours of winter. On all sides the oaks stood gaunt and grey, rising from dark undercrofts of holly. But on the woodland floor, among the acid gleams of moss and unkempt acres of rusted bracken, primroses were flowering, and already the bluebell leaves were spearing through the leaf litter.

It was mid-March, the sky a watercolour wash pierced by broken panes of blue. The wind was cold but there was no malice in it, and when it stopped I could hear a mistle thrush singing deeper in the woods.

The smell of spring was in the air, conjuring up Philip Larkin's poem about the trees coming into leaf 'like something being said'. In places along the well-trodden path from Bolderwood Bridge the sour woodland soil had been churned to the consistency of a buffalo wallow by deer, ponies and the boots of walkers. But farther on, after the path had swung away from the river, the footing was firmer.

From here it was easy walking, crunching over gravel for most of the way to Pinkney Lane, which led past a house with a wrought-iron roe-deer weathervane into the perfect New Forest hamlet of Bank, at the southwestern approaches to Lyndhurst.

The trick here is to plan your arrival in time for lunch at the Oak Inn, an archetypal New Forest pub with garlands of dried hops over the bar and fishing rods hanging from its oak-beamed ceilings. I sat in a corner with a ham sandwich and a half-pint of Adnams, beneath a faded photograph of Henry 'Brusher' Mills, the legendary New Forest snake-catcher, who lived in a charcoal-burner's hut and sold adders to London Zoo for a shilling. He died in 1905, aged sixty-five, and is buried in Brockenhurst churchyard.

Afterwards, having back-tracked down Pinkney Lane to the house with the weathervane, I rejoined the forest path and emerged in a broad glade rimmed with birches, where New Forest ponies were grazing in a sea of heather.

Farther on, having crossed the A337 at the southern edge of Lyndhurst, I came to the woods of Park Ground Inclosure. 'First inclosed in 1810', said the sign on the gate. These inclosures – plantations enclosed by a stock-proof fence – are managed for timber production. Many have been planted with dark stands of conifers and are quite different in character to the so-called 'Ancient and Ornamental Woodlands', where conservation is paramount and the deer and ponies come and go as they please.

Nevertheless, the enclosed plantations, stitched together by a maze of rides, offer agreeable walking and solitude. On the entire stretch back to Brockenhurst by way of Standing Hat and Balmer Lawn I met only two people – mountain bikers bound for Lyndhurst.

Next day, having stayed the night in Brockenhurst, I had organised a taxi to take me to Beaulieu, six miles away, for a Sunday stroll down the Solent Way footpath.

The Solent Way hugs the Channel coast from Milford on Sea to Lymington, then turns inland towards Beaulieu and runs on across Beaulieu Heath to Hythe Pier on the shores of Southampton Water, where it continues on the opposite shore and links up with the Itchen Way. The section I was following, from Beaulieu to Buckler's Hard on the Beaulieu River, was just a taste: little more than a couple of miles between the woods and the water, but enough to make me want to come back and walk the whole path.

At Buckler's Hard the riverside echoed to the mindless jangling of wire rigging slapping in the wind against a forest of yacht masts. In the boatyard, rows of polished hulls – *Admiral Thomas, Holly Blue, Nomad of Beaulieu* and *Illusion* among them – were being given their last lick of paint before the sailing season started.

It was strange to think that these wide reaches have their beginnings back in the forest only a mile or two from Lyndhurst. There, the river is little more than a trickle in a gravel ditch among the trees. Here it was a fully fledged tideway, smelling strongly of the sea.

In the Buckler's Hard Maritime Museum I wandered among rows of glass cases filled with cutlasses and flintlock pistols, relics of Lord Nelson, and the tools of the men who built his fighting ships out of New Forest oaks. In all, twenty-nine of Nelson's fleet were launched from the stocks at Buckler's Hard, including his favourites, the sixty-four-gun *Agamemnon* and the thirty-six-gun *Euryalus*, both of which fought at Trafalgar.

An oak must grow for a hundred years before it can be felled for shipbuilding, and the demands of the Navy were even more than the New Forest alone could fulfil; yet local trees provided much of the valuable 'compass' timber – the stout posts and curved ribs that could be shaped with minimum effort from the oak's crooked branches. It took two thousand mature trees to build the *Agamemnon* in 1781; and by 1805 – the year of Trafalgar – there were perhaps one and a half million oaks afloat in the service of the Royal Navy.

Nearby, at the Master Builder's House Hotel, Sunday lunchtime smells were wafting from what in Nelson's day was the home of

Henry Adams, master shipwright, but I had planned to walk back to Beaulieu and spend the rest of the day at the National Motor Museum in the grounds of Palace House, Lord Montagu's sixteenth-century home.

An odd choice, ending a walking weekend in a shrine to the motorcar? Maybe; but it also underlines the versatility of the New Forest. After all, where else in Britain can you step from the motor age back into the timeless hush of William the Conqueror's wildwood?

Mayfly

River Test, Hampshire, May 1988

If I were an exile pining for England, May is the month I would miss the most.

The return of summer: cuckoos calling, hawthorn blossom bursting like Atlantic surf along the hedgerows and yellowhammers wheezing from the telephone wires in the long light evenings.

At home the lanes are choked with cow parsley, lit by the lily-white bells of ramsons, by whose thick garlic breath I could recognise West Dorset with my eyes shut. The swifts are back from Africa, screaming over the rooftops and seeming none the worse for having spent the past nine months entirely on the wing.

With them has come another fast and dashing flier, itself not unlike a large swift. The hobby is a beautiful sickle-winged falcon, moustachioed like a Mexican bandit, with rust-red leg feathers and a taste for dragonflies that it grabs in the air and eats on the wing. It spends the winter deep in Tanzania, hunting over the Rufiji delta and the Maasai steppe; but in May it returns to breed in southern England, striking terror among our resident swallows and martin colonies whenever its rakish silhouette cuts through the sky.

Yet for all its élan and predatory glamour, the month belongs not to the piratical hobby but to an altogether more delicate creature with gossamer wings. For May is traditionally the month to witness the most spectacular uprising in the insect calendar. It happens with almost stopwatch precision and there is no better place to see it than from the banks of a Hampshire chalk stream.

The Test is such a river – possibly not the world's finest trout stream, but undoubtedly the most famous. For anglers, every inch of its banks is hallowed ground. There are salmon in the lower reaches, but higher up the trout is king – both native brown and stocked rainbow.

Between the mares' tails of water crowfoot, in the long swims where the water runs bright over clean gravel, the river is alive with their hovering shadows. And here, around the fifteenth of the month – certainly no later than the nineteenth – the season is marked by one of the last great natural phenomena of the English countryside, as the river's surface shivers and dissolves beneath a mass of dancing mayflies.

The mayfly is easily the largest of the Ephemeroptera order – aquatic insects with delicate wings like leaded windows. From the head to the tip of its triple cat's-whisker tail it measures close on two inches and, at rest, clinging to the underside of a leaf, its wings are pressed together like hands in prayer above the slender body.

The mayfly spends the first two years of its life as an underwater nymph, whiskered and unlovely, burrowing in the silt and breathing through gills on its back. But in May it crawls to the surface and undergoes a dramatic double metamorphosis, emerging first as a dun, or sub-imago with dull wings, and finally as the adult fly, glistening and complete, rising and falling over the water in the throes of its mating dance.

Often the dance begins with a mere sprinkling of flies; but sometimes, as when unfavourable weather holds back the hatch, the pent-up insects take to the air in dense cumulus clouds.

True to their scientific name, mayflies lead ephemeral lives. Two or three days at most and they are done. Once mated, the massed females return to the water to lay their eggs and die. To the waiting trout the spent flies must appear like snowflakes on a windowpane. Now begins a time of plenty – 'duffer's fortnight' – when even the most inept angler can hook a trout as the fish rise and rise again to suck down the dead and dying insects with a faint but audible smack of the lips.

Even without the annual miracle of the mayflies, the Test is remarkable: for much of its modest length it is very private, its exclusive beats and fishing huts closed off by privilege, so that often it reveals itself as no more than a tantalising gleam far out in the water meadows or a receding perspective of bankside trees.

It is not a wild river like the Tay, or a rolling river like the Severn. It lacks the limestone crags of the Dove, the Wye's wooded symmetry. The Test is a chalk stream, pure and simple, and, in May, when the waters begin to run gin-clear and its galleon reaches of great willows stand becalmed in a sea of buttercups, time and place come together to distil the essence of a southern English summer.

This is an active time for all river life. Other insects besides mayflies appear. Prominent among them are glossy black hawthorn flies with long trailing legs. Orange-tip butterflies search the meadows for lady's smock, and metallic green demoiselle flies rest on the crowfoot's floating tresses. Long before sunrise the banks are loud with the harsh song of reed warblers whose cup-shaped nests, slung between the tall *Phragmites* stems, will soon hold green-speckled eggs.

By early evening the river is like smoked glass. Rising trout dimple its surface, leaving a few bubbles to ride past on the swirling current. A cuckoo calls across the meadows. Warmth and windless air lull the senses. It is all so peaceful, inalienable and unchanging.

Yet even this sacred valley is no longer immune to the forces that have been reshaping so much of our countryside. Here as elsewhere, inch by aquatic inch the mayfly is losing ground. Outwardly the Test is as serene as ever, but under the surface something slow and insidious is at work.

Causes and theories abound: rising nitrate levels, insecticides washed from the fields, trout-farm slurry, dredging and drainage schemes that disturb the riverbed in which the mayfly nymphs live. All may take their toll. Mayflies need shade and shelter, and the remorseless defoliation of the farmed landscape – the removal of trees, hedges and bankside cover – may also be hastening their decline.

If the mayfly goes, how long will it be before the trout and the swifts and reed warblers follow? In the fight to maintain our clean rivers, the dance of the mayflies is a welcome sign that the battle is not yet lost.

The Secret Life of the Fox

Wytham Woods, Oxfordshire, January 1988

The mist clears slowly from these cold Oxfordshire clay farmlands. The sky is sullen with the threat of snow and the remaining hours of daylight will not shift last night's frost.

Ahead lie Wytham Woods, brooding on their hilltop like a dreadful secret, and somewhere in there a-hunting we will go, although not with hounds or guns but with earphones and radio antennae. Wire-tappers in muddy boots, we are sneaking down Wytham's gloomy rides to eavesdrop on the private life of the fox.

For fifteen years David Macdonald, zoologist, author and fox-watcher extraordinary, has been tracking the foxes of Oxfordshire to unravel the mysteries surrounding Britain's most misunderstood predator. His quest has taken him from the upwardly mobile foxes of the affluent suburbs to the streetwise foxes of Oxford city, and far beyond the hunting shires to the lean hill foxes of the Cumbrian fells.

It was no easy task. Centuries of persecution have taught foxes to shun man like the plague. By day, mere fleeting shadows. By night, only a spine-tingling shriek in the dark.

To stay with the fox called for single-minded dedication bordering on the obsessive, but Macdonald persevered. Gradually he began to see the countryside as it must appear to the fox: not as a planned mosaic of fields, lanes and hedgerows, but as a pungent world of tracks and scent marks, good mouse-hunting grounds, safe earths and snug lying up places. And all the time he was unearthing fresh facts about the creature hidden behind that keen-eyed mask.

We park in a clearing beneath a giant Spanish chestnut. I haven't a clue where I am, but Macdonald would know these eight hundred acres blindfold. The woods are not open to the public except by special permission. Instead, for more than half a century, Wytham has been a living laboratory in which generations of university students have pursued their PhDs, studying everything from oaks to bluetits.

The woods are held in a deep-frozen silence, but signs of life are everywhere: deer tracks, badger trails. The woodland floor is also covered with an all-but-invisible web of fox paths; an olfactory landscape laced with rank foxy smells.

At the end of the ride is a wreckage of pigeon feathers. Macdonald picks up a handful of primaries. The chewed quills are clearly the mark of a fox. Had the pigeon been killed by a sparrowhawk they would have been plucked, not bitten.

The pigeon must have been a welcome change from the earthworms that are a major part of the fox's diet. Foxes are also partial to beetles, blackberries, windfall apples, household scraps and bread put out for the birds. In fact there's not much a fox won't eat.

On the whole estate, reckons Macdonald, there may be ten fox families. Each family consists of between three and five adults with a territory of some 250 acres that is divided between the woods and the adjoining farmlands.

The idea of the fox as a loner is just one of the myths that Macdonald's work has dispelled and it would have been impossible without the aid of radio tracking. 'For field biologists it's the revolution of the century,' he says, 'the greatest invention since binoculars.'

The idea is simple. First catch your fox. Then fit it with a dog collar to which is attached a radio transmitter, matchbox size, rather like a St Bernard with a brandy keg. When the fox is released it sends out a constant signal that can be picked up by the fox-watcher.

In the wood's hollow heart a robin sings the day to rest. Three fallow deer break cover in front of us. They clear the ride in a single bound and vanish among the trees.

Macdonald stalks on. He hates the cold, he says, suffers dreadfully from frozen feet and is far happier tracking meerkats in the Kalahari; but his heart is with the fox in these bleak midwinter landscapes.

Suddenly he stops. He has picked up a signal, a regular bleeping on his receiver. The wavelength tells him it's the vixen, Broken Tooth. She is lying up no more than fifty yards away. Macdonald knows the place well: an overgrown clearing among the leafless oaks. There, impervious to the frost in her thick winter coat, she'll be curled up in a thicket.

This is her third winter. She is one of a family of four, a non-breeding adult waiting to inherit the mating hierarchy from an older vixen known as Pod. Her range extends from the woods across ten fields and includes a farm rubbish tip that yields an endless supply of rats.

It seems that three is a ripe age for a fox. With a yearly mortality rate of around sixty per cent, foxes lead fleeting lives, as Macdonald graphically explains. 'Fox society is like ours would be if most of us died aged twenty-one.'

With dusk coming down a fox begins to call in the woods. It's the sharp triple bark that means 'I am here, where are you?'

Almost at once it brings a response, like the echo if its own voice returning. Broken Tooth's friends are coming to call.

Now blackbirds are sending their chinking alarm calls along the edge of the woods. A flock of wood pigeons clatter into the sky. And suddenly a fox steps out into the field.

It's impossible to tell if it is Broken Tooth. For a moment it stands motionless, sifting the air for scent and sound. Then it is trotting, a quick brown shadow flitting through the furrows on feet that hardly seem to touch the ground. The night of the fox is here.

In the hours to come the woods will ring to the excited barking of dog foxes and the unearthly scream of courting vixens. For January is the month when vulpine urges peak, reaching a noisy crescendo in the last few nights before February, and it's a comforting thought that, in the cold, dead heart of winter, conception in an Oxfordshire wood will bring new life in March when the cubs are born.

WEST AND WALES

In early summer the wild spirit of the hills is heard in the voices of the curlews. The birds fly up from solitary places above their beloved and little ones, and float the wind in a sweet uprising music. Slowly on spread and hollow wings they sink, and their cries are trilling and cadent, until they touch earth and lift their wings above their heads, and poising, loose the last notes from their throats, like gold bubbles rising to the sky again.

from Tarka the Otter *by Henry Williamson*

Tarka Territory

Georgeham, Devon, June 1997

'The stream flowed below a churchyard wall and by a thatched cottage where a man, a dog and a cat were sitting before a fire of elm brands on the open hearth. The wind blew the scent of the otter under the door and the cat fumed and growled, standing with fluffed back and twitching tail beside her basket of kittens.'

In the North Devon village of Georgeham, the cottage still stands beside the stream, but the man who lived there and wrote those words now lies in the churchyard beneath a simple slate slab inscribed with the image of a barn owl. Henry Williamson died in 1977, but *Tarka the Otter*, his 'joyful water-life and death in the Country of the Two Rivers', remains the greatest nature classic in English literature. More than any other writer since Hardy, he caught the spirit of a special corner of England and made it his own.

Williamson country lies between Exmoor and Dartmoor, where two Devon rivers, the Taw and Torridge, emerge from their deep wooded valleys to meet the Atlantic in a vast estuary of salt marsh, dunes and sandbars. Williamson knew and loved every inch of it; and even now, with a map, you can follow his footsteps through the printed pages.

Henry Williamson was born in London in 1895. In 1914 he joined the army and fought on the Western Front until, traumatically, he was sent home badly shell-shocked and suffering from dysentery.

After the war he worked in London as a freelance journalist, but city life proved too much for his shattered nerves. In 1921 he climbed onto his 499cc BRS Norton motorbike and headed for a new life in North Devon.

In Georgeham he rented Skirr Cottage, a cob-and-thatch labourer's dwelling built in the days of King John. He paid eighteen pence a week and inherited a family of barn owls that nested above the ceiling. The barn owl at once became his totem, its outline picked out in paint on his cottage door.

Apart from the birds, his only companions were dogs, cats and at one stage an otter cub whose mother had been shot. Williamson persuaded his cat – already nursing a kitten – to suckle the cub, and the young otter took to following him on long walks around the countryside. But their relationship ended one evening when the animal stepped in a gin trap. By the time Williamson managed to release it, the trap had almost severed three of the otter's toes. Utterly terrified, it wriggled from his grasp and vanished.

He never saw his otter again, but the idea of *Tarka* had been born, and in 1923 he began to write. Soon afterwards he was married, a son was born and the family moved to Crowberry Cottage, just a few doors down the road from Skirr. And it was here, having been laboriously revised seventeen times, that *Tarka* was finished in 1927. It won him the Hawthornden Prize. 'A hundred pounds and fame,' he cried on hearing the news, and spent the money on a field at Ox's Cross, near Georgeham, where his elm-board writing hut still stands.

By the time he was seventy-four he had completed two sprawling sagas – *The Flax of Dreams* and *A Chronicle of Ancient Sunlight*, an immense fifteen-volume canvas stretching from the turn of the nineteenth century across two world wars. It should have assured him a place among the greatest English writers of the age, but none of his later work ever achieved the lasting impact of *Tarka*.

The writer Kenneth Allsop believed Williamson was a genius. 'I think I can be objective about expressing this judgement of him,' he wrote, 'because in fact his political philosophy could hardly be more different from my personal outlook on man and society.' And yet Williamson was to die unhonoured, a loner to the end and, but for *Tarka*, almost forgotten.

'*Tarka*'s fame irritated Henry,' said Daniel Farson, Williamson's biographer and friend for a quarter of a century, 'and yet he was also immensely proud of it.' Farson was still in his teens when they first met, and he remembered Henry in those days as 'a lean, vibrant, almost quivering man with blazing mesmeric eyes' (which is how I, too, remember him when we met in Dorset shortly before his death).

I met Farson in Appledore, where he had lived for the past twelve years in a converted boat-builder's loft overlooking the estuary. 'They were idyllic days,' he said, describing the summers of the late 1940s. Yet even by 1953, as Farson's biography of Williamson records, Henry was already lamenting the changes that had overwhelmed Appledore. 'Paper, Wall's ice cream cartons, shrieking children. A polluted estuary; a million-pound electric coal station erected over the water on the snipe bogs that once were. The Burrows are a tank ground now.'

In the 1920s Williamson could still write about the 'wild, beautiful, unexplored Atlantic seaboard; the falcons, the otters, the badgers, the salmon, the character of the people', as if Devon were another country. It was a time when farmers in early spring would stamp out into the soft West Country dawns to plough their fields with heavy horses, when pigs were killed outside cottage doors, squealing as their blood gushed into bowls for 'bloody pie'. Across the estuary in Appledore, among the cobbled alleys and sawdust-smelling boatyards, you might still find old 'mast-and-yards' men who had served their sea time aboard square-rigged sailing ships. And it was not uncommon even then to see a three-masted schooner waiting for the flood tide to carry her up to Bideford with a cargo of Baltic timber.

Williamson was writing in the sunset of English rural life. In the villages the old order, shaken to its roots by the Great War, would never be the same. Only when you compare his vivid descriptions with the reality of the present is it possible to measure the changes that have overtaken, and in places overwhelmed, North Devon.

Fifteen elms stood in the churchyard when Williamson first came to Georgeham. Rooks nested in their tall canopies and barn owls emerged from the roof of Skirr Cottage to hunt among the gravestones. Now, the trees are gone – victims of Dutch elm disease – and barn owls are scarcer everywhere. At the upper end of the village the seventeenth-century Rock Inn now bears little resemblance to the pub of Williamson's era, when men in waistcoats and collarless shirts drank Barnstaple bitter from china mugs and sang in a haze of tobacco smoke.

Yet for Williamson's son, Richard, Georgeham was not so different from the village he remembered from his boyhood. 'There was more cow shit in the streets in those days,' he said. 'The smell of cows was everywhere. Little black cars, fewer buildings, that's what I remember. But still the same old lanes, the same stone walls.

The only real change is the orange glow of the street lights from the new estate.'

On the hill above Georgeham, where four lanes meet at Ox's Cross, Williamson's elm-board writing hut still looks out across the immense sweep of Bideford Bay. The strange, Ibsenesque house he added in the 1970s has been sold out of the family, but the hut remains, standing under the pines he planted well over half a century ago.

Those were the days when you could walk down to the estuary and be rowed across to Appledore for a shilling. It is all holiday coast now. Saunton and Putsborough Sands surrendered long ago to the surfers and sunbathers, and the summer lanes are choked with traffic heading for the beaches. Only Baggy Point survives untouched – a wild National Trust headland where the Atlantic bursts with thunderous force against lichen-scabbed cliffs.

To the south lies Dartmoor, where the Taw rises among desolate bogs under Hangingstone Hill. In its upper reaches the Taw is a typical Dartmoor stream, spilling over mossy boulders in a chain of amber pools. By the time it has left Belstone Cleave and slid beneath the A30 at Sticklepath it is already deep enough to hide a salmon. Downstream below King's Nympton, diesel trains rumble over iron-girdered bridges that Williamson knew in the age of steam, but here at least in the lush valley farmlands, the Taw is timeless. It remains the Gentlemen's River – so called by the old otter hunters, who knew that wherever they stopped for refreshments they would never be far from a riverside inn.

Life for Britain's otters has always been precarious. Until the Great War they were persecuted by gamekeepers and water bailiffs. Then the keepers went off to fight and the otters multiplied. Britain was never again so heavily keepered, and in the ancient, unpolluted countryside that existed between the wars, otters flourished as never before.

They continued to thrive until 1957, when their numbers suddenly plummeted. The cause was pesticides – the same persistent chemicals that were simultaneously bringing about the decline of the sparrowhawk and the peregrine falcon. Eventually the more harmful pesticides – Dieldrin and DDT for example – were banned, and so, eventually, was otter hunting. In 1978 the otter was given full protection under the Conservation of Wild Creatures Act. Sadly it came too late and was not enough to halt the slide. While birds of prey recovered well, the otter vanished from most of its English haunts. Only in the Southwest, on the Taw and Torridge river systems, have numbers increased since 1977, and even here they are still in danger.[1]

Ironically, it was the otter hunters who first raised the alarm over the animal's disappearance. 'Conservationists would never have been aware that otters were in trouble if it hadn't been for the hunters getting worried over the declining numbers,' said Don Jefferies, one of the Nature Conservancy Council's mammal experts.

The Masters of Otter Hounds Association brought in its own voluntary ban on killing otters in the early 1970s and, when legal protection came, most hunts disbanded altogether. Others such as the Dartmoor renamed themselves – in the Dartmoor's case as the Devon and Cornwall – and re-emerged to pursue the mink that had begun to infest Britain's rivers. Many mink hunts used fox hounds,

---

[1] Otters have made such a steady comeback that they are now widespread again in Britain and present in every English county.

but the Devon and Cornwall still kept the real old-fashioned otter hounds, with traditional names such as Capital and Bellman, Songster and Solemn. 'Such lovely animals,' said Arlin Rickard, a former hunt master. 'Stocky and heavy-boned, with thick coats and webbed feet. As a breed they were even rarer than the otter.'

The Cheriton, which pursued Tarka on the Taw and Torridge, had already ceased hunting by 1945 and survived only as a club. But the neighbouring mink hunts were still invited to the Cheriton country, and on certain days between May and September the Valleys of the Two Rivers still rang to the deep-throated belling of the hounds, as if haunted by Deadlock's ghost.

Nowhere in the Country of the Two Rivers is the atmosphere of Williamson's Devon richer than on the banks of the Torridge. It's an odd river, rising within a few miles of the Atlantic near Hartland Point, but then perversely turning its back on the sea and running inland towards Dartmoor. There once more it changes its mind and meanders past Dipper Mill and Sheepwash, then loops down through high hills and hanging woods to Great Torrington and Weare Giffard before running out into the estuary beyond Bideford.

For much of its thirty-four miles, especially in its upper reaches above Torrington, the Torridge is a secret river. Sometimes, while cruising down the web of back lanes that crisscross this corner of the county, you catch a tantalising glimpse of it, sliding past like polished glass under bankside oaks, or running bright over stony shillets between summertime jungles of invasive Himalayan balsam. But most of the time it shuns the roads, losing itself in the woods and water meadows of a landscape hardly changed since Williamson's time.

Now, as then, what the visitor sees is a time-warp countryside of herons and buttercups in which Beam Weir and Halfpenny Bridge – familiar scenes in *Tarka* – remain just as when the book was written. Even vanished landmarks have been brought back to life. Below Canal Bridge, thirteen gnarled trees once stood with their roots in the river. In one was Owlery Holt – Tarka's birthplace. All are gone, but thirteen new trees now stand in their place, planted by the Vincent Wildlife Trust.

'For me that whole area around Weare Giffard shrieks of Tarka,' said David Cobham, the director who filmed the story in 1977 and got to know Williamson well in his last years. 'Henry even looked like an otter, with his bristly moustache and piercing brown eyes.'

By the strangest coincidence, Cobham was filming the death of Tarka on the day Henry died. It was a glorious day in Devon on 13 August 1977, and Cobham kept on filming until early evening. The final shot, with the three bubbles rising after Deadlock is drowned and Tarka is carried away on the outgoing tide, was completed just as the light was beginning to fade. Next day Richard Williamson told him, 'I thought you should know that while you were filming Tarka's death scene yesterday, Henry died.' Cobham was stunned. 'It gave me a very prickly feeling,' he said. 'It seemed almost predestined.'

In recent years an entire local tourist industry has gathered itself around Williamson's famous otter. The Tarka Project, a Devon County Council initiative, now actively promotes sustainable tourism in the region with a Tarka Trail – a 180-mile footpath – opened by Prince Charles in May 1992.

Among those who advised on setting up the Tarka Trail was Trevor Beer, a local writer, and it was he who took me to Braunton Burrows, the sea of dunes that lies to the north of the estuary behind Saunton Sands. He remembers meeting Williamson there one winter. 'It was a cold day and the old man's eyes were watering. His heavy coat was pulled about his shoulders, which were normally straight but now hunched against the wind.' Characteristically, Williamson broke off the conversation to shake his fist at a low-flying jet from RAF Chivenor.

We parked near the solitary white house on Crow Point and sat on the sea wall by Horsey Marsh as the sun burned down and moorhens hiccupped in the mace-reeds. The sands below the sea wall are still as Williamson described them, except that now, on top of the shells of razor-fish and cockles, dried seaweed thongs and bleached driftwood, our own age had added an oily flotsam of plastic bottles.

Behind the highest tide-lines, the Burrows rise in a shaggy crest of marram grass. It is an extraordinary place, an English Kalahari, three thousand acres of wind-blown hills owned by the Christie Estate. The greater part is leased to the Ministry of Defence for military training, though in its turn it has been leased to English Nature as a biosphere reserve.

'One time I went down there looking for whitethroats,' said Beer, 'and commandos armed to the teeth popped up out of the dunes.' But on the whole the military and the conservationists have managed to coexist in an uneasy equilibrium – exemplified by the thrush Beer watched smashing snails on an unexploded shell.

In summer the Burrows are hot and breathless. The sand burns underfoot. The dunes quiver in the dazzling Atlantic light. The sea wind hisses through the marram, bearing the sound of skylarks and the boom of surf breaking on Bideford Bar. But below the wind, among the mossy slacks and damp hollows, the surf is muted and the dunes are thick with flowers: wild orchids, yellow spires of evening primrose and the vivid blue of viper's bugloss.

It would be foolish to imagine that North Devon has not changed in half a century, or that rural life was better in Williamson's day. Towns and villages are bigger. Roads are busier, beaches crowded. Noise, power lines and pollution have all conspired to diminish its beauty. Yet the Land of the Two Rivers remains its own place, stubborn and inward-looking. In spite of everything, the magic survives – in the Burrows, in the shape of the coast, the lie of the land, its ancient geometry of fields, woods and crooked hedge banks.

The power station that defiled Williamson's beloved snipe bogs has been demolished. The jets he hated have left RAF Chivenor. The peregrines have returned to their Atlantic eyries and, best of all, the Torridge has been cleaned up and reborn. Once again it has become a river fit for otters where, long ago, a shell-shocked survivor from the trenches sought refuge in the country with an orphaned cub and found immortality.

Sand as Soft as Talc

Isles of Scilly, April 1989

One day in spring, when the Isles of Scilly were the warmest place in Britain, I walked over the white sand causeway from St Agnes to Gugh. The sun shone from a cloudless sky and I sat on a rock and listened to the first cuckoo calling across a blissful silence of gorse and granite. The sea was an intense blue, shot through with sharp emerald gleams where sand lay beneath the shallows between the deep indigo shadows of submerged reefs and kelp beds.

Nearby, on a beach as soft as talc, the last of the winter storms had flung up the bleached bones of a seal, that rested now in the marram grass, together with a scattering of mauve mussel shells, dried seaweed and odd bits of driftwood. A flock of oystercatchers with coral-red bills were piping at the tide's edge. Otherwise the only footprints in the sand were mine.

Forget the Maldives, the Seychelles and the Grenadines. The Isles of Scilly are only thirty miles from Land's End, but they lie out in the Gulf Stream where frosts are rare and sunfish bask in summer. There are no snakes or mosquitoes, no muggers or robbers. Fly from Land's End and you can be at St Mary's in fifteen minutes.

Heathrow it isn't. You touch down in a daisy field, as effortlessly as a gull on a roof, and step out into a luminous, sea-girt world that looks like the Cornwall of sixty years ago. Breathe deep. The salty Scillonian air will rot a car in three years, but it is wonderfully pure and a joy to inhale – distilled over two thousand miles of ocean by Atlantic breezes that bring unusual and exotic birds to the islands:

nighthawks and magnolia warblers from America, hoopoes and orioles from Southern Europe.

Out of the wind, the climate is kind. While the rest of Britain shivers in the grip of winter, the Scillonians are busy in their pocket-sized bulb fields, cutting daffodils for the London market. By springtime, parts of the islands are as luxuriant as the Mediterranean. Palm trees sprout from cottage gardens. Bees drone among giant azure spires of echiums from the Canaries. On St Mary's I saw a blue field, like a Picasso painting: a solid carpet of Spanish bluebells. Other fields are bright with Bermuda buttercups and whistling jacks – wild red gladioli from Africa once grown commercially but now gone native, rooted among the more familiar West Country wild flowers.

When my roving days are over, this is where I, too, would be happy to put down my roots, in a small granite house, snug under the sea wind, with a garden full of daffodils and a view of the bluest sea this side of the Caribbean. On Bryher I met a man who has done just that. Mac Mace is a professional diver from Nottingham who has successfully transplanted himself to this, the smallest of Scilly's five inhabited islands, where he and Tracy, his wife, run a guesthouse. The sea begins at his garden gate. From his lounge he can point out the site of twenty-two shipwrecks. Indoors is a signal cannon retrieved from the wreck of Admiral Sir Cloudesley Shovell's flagship, HMS *Association*. 'Possibly the last gun she fired before she struck on the Gilstone Ledge on a stormy October night in 1707,' says Mace.

'She was a ninety-six-gun ship of the line and she was carrying the Queen's plate, ten chests of Sir Cloudesley's own and great riches of the grandees of Spain. Now she's lying in a hundred-feet-deep valley, scattered across a seabed of cottage-size boulders. You can see the snouts of her cannons, but the gold and silver coin and other artefacts have dribbled down between the rocks. Getting at them is more like mining than diving.'

Yet, little by little, the *Association* is yielding up her treasure: English silver coins welded together by centuries of corrosion; Portuguese gold pieces as bright as the day they were minted. Last year Mace found an apricot stone, which he almost persuaded to germinate; and, most poignant of all, a sailor's gold ring inscribed with the words 'In thy breast my heart does rest.'

On a sunny day the waters around Bryher are idyllic, a maze of ledges and gull-haunted islets threaded by glittering turquoise channels. One stretch has the most beautiful name in Scilly: the Garden of Maiden Bower. But how different it is in a big winter storm, when Hell Bay seethes like scalded milk and the roaring seas break clean over the outlying rock castles of Mincarlo.

Mac Mace knows well the unimaginable power of the sea. Once he dived on the ill-fated tanker *Torrey Canyon*, wrecked on the Seven Stones reef in 1967. 'She's huge, an eleven-storey hull of solid iron,' he says. 'Yet the sea has shoved her along the bottom for more than a hundred yards since she went down.'

He is equally knowledgeable about Bryher, knows every inch of its three hundred acres of yellow gorse and Iron Age cairns. 'Look,' he cries, sinking to his knees to identify a blue pinhead in the grass. It turns out to be a rare miniature violet which, he says, grows only here and on Jersey.

'People come to Bryher and ask us what there is to do, and we tell them there's nothing. That's the joy of it, that and a sense of man having lived here for three thousand years.'

On Bryher, as elsewhere in the Scillies, such joys are synonymous with peace and tranquillity. Even on St Mary's, where locals complain about the island's three hundred cars, traffic has a minimal presence. Boats are far more important, and every morning a stream of launches sets out from St Mary's Quay to deposit visitors on the off-islands for the day. The finest beaches are on St Martin's, and at certain times of the year, when the tide runs out and the sea light pours across the shining sands, you can walk barefoot from Bryher to Tresco, more than half a mile away, without ever wading more than knee deep.

In April 1989 a new hotel opened on St Martin's, a rare event in the Scillies, and one that inevitably aroused a degree of acrimony among the island's eighty inhabitants. Yet, as a visitor, I can only say that its modest slate and granite proportions sit happily on the shores of Tean Sound, no more conspicuous than a row of coastguard cottages, and I know of no other hotel in Britain, and few elsewhere, with lovelier seascape views.

Tresco, most popular of the off-islands, is a private paradise owned by the Dorrien-Smith family, whose eccentric ancestor, Augustus 'Emperor' Smith, created the subtropical gardens of Tresco Abbey more than a century ago. The Scillies are renowned for their mild winters, but in January 1987 the unthinkable happened when the inhabitants of Tresco awoke to find everything buried under six inches of snow. For the Abbey Gardens it was a disaster. It was so cold that the sap froze in the trees and many tender plants were lost. Even today the windbreak hedges of high pittosporum stand grey and stricken around the bulb fields. But at Tresco Abbey the gardens have made a miraculous recovery and remain among the wonders of Britain. This is a closed world of rockroses and goldfinch song, drowsy and sun-warmed, steeped in the incense of Monterey pines, its granite terraces overwhelmed by cascades of pink mesembryanthemums and Madeira geraniums.

Here, too, is Tresco's extraordinary Valhalla of shipwreck figureheads. Gilded and ghostly white, they fly out of the shadows as if they were still cleaving the wild Atlantic. There are golden lions, blue dolphins, a Highland chieftain and a Puritan maid. But the loveliest and most enigmatic by far is a brown-eyed wench with a comb in her hair – the Spanish Lady – salvaged from a mystery vessel dashed upon the Scilly rocks.

Back in Hugh Town, I bought a wreck chart of the Scillies produced by Roland Morris of Penzance, every inch of it littered with the names of dead ships: barques and brigantines, East Indiamen and great ships of the line, clippers bound for Falmouth for orders, Dutch galliots, French crabbers, proud schooners and humble steam trawlers. It is a chilling document, a roll call of the deep, listing the hundreds of ships lost and men drowned in these islands over the centuries. But it is also a vivid testimonial to the romance of sea travel, a geography and history lesson in one.

It lists cargoes of fustic and indigo, tea from Foochow, coal from Cardiff, and each terse entry tells a story. 'The ship *Polinarus*, on passage from Demerara to London with rum and sugar, lost with all hands, 1848… the SS *Schiller*, wrecked on the Retarrier Ledges with the loss of more than 300 lives… the *Louise Hannah* from Lisbon to her home port of Poole with oranges and wine, lost off Annet, all hands lost, 1839.'

And listen to the names of the rocks that sent them to the bottom: Tearing Ledge, the Hellweathers, Great Wingletang, the Gunners, the Beast and the infamous Gilstone.

Who sank the Association?
I, said the Gilstone,
She sank like a millstone.

Next day I went out to the Western Rocks to visit some of these unrepentant old murderers. The boat rose and fell among the hills of blue water. Shell-bursts of spray blossomed against the Haycocks, too far away to hear, and the Bishop Rock lighthouse stood pencil-slim on its solitary pinnacle like an admonishing finger.

What courage it must have taken to live there, marooned among those fearsome deeps, knowing that the first lighthouse to be built on the Bishop was washed away in a storm.

Puffins whirred from beneath our bows, and grey seals with sleek mottled bodies and wistful eyes slipped into the water as we nosed among the reefs of Rosevean and Melledgan. Even on a calm day the sea is never still. The tide sucks constantly at the barnacled granite, swilling around the tusks and teeth of those grim ledges to subside with a sinister gasp, like the last breath of a drowning sailor. You think of all the fine ships that have come to grief here, and the sunless silence of the kelp forests below, and pray the weather holds.

On my last morning, as cloudless as the first, I rented a bike in Hugh Town and went freewheeling down the empty lanes to the sea. The day stretched before me and I felt as carefree as a child. Where the road ended, I left the bike among the bluebells, knowing nobody would steal it, and set out along the coast path to Porth Hellick. The scent of the gorse rolled in thick coconut tides across the cliff tops. The sea lay glassy calm. Out on the horizon beyond Great Arthur, the faint smudge of a ship caught my eye. I stared at it through my binoculars in disbelief. It was a ghost ship, a dream from the past: a great square-rigger under full sail.

That evening she lay at anchor in the seaway known as St Mary's Road. She was the *Belem*, a French sail-training ship homeward bound for Nantes. But for me, her masts and shrouds deep-etched against the dying golden light, she was a haunting echo from a century ago, when these perilous waters were the crossroads of the world and the swift, six-oared Scillonian pilot gigs – *Shah, Bonnet, Golden Eagle* – rowed out between the Western Rocks to guide the tall ships safely home.

Where the Land Runs Out

West Penwith, Cornwall, June 1997

In West Penwith at the toe end of Cornwall, everything is granite, from the moors above to the cliffs below. It is the key to understanding the obdurate nature of these rain-washed parishes whose inhabitants still live in granite farmhouses, sail out from granite harbours and worship in granite churches as they have done for a thousand years.

Life here has always been a struggle, fishing and farming in the eye of the wind or wresting tin and copper from deep shafts that, in places, run out for a mile or more under the seabed. The narrow roads, the unyielding hedge banks, the remoteness that comes with being an extremity – all have conspired to hold back the forces that have been relentlessly smothering the rest of England under a creeping blanket of Home Counties culture.

This was the Cornwall that attracted generations of painters to Newlyn and St Ives, lured by the brilliance of the light flung up from its encircling seas. St Ives may have changed, but West Penwith is timeless. Like sand in an hourglass, everything that is most Cornish about Cornwall has settled here. West Penwith is Cornwall's last stand. Even a cursory glance at the map shows this to be no ordinary corner of Britain. The Cornish language was finally snuffed out when Dolly Pentreath, its last speaker, died in Mousehole in 1777, but Penwith's weird place names – Skewjack, Crows-an-wra, Polgigga, Woon Gumpus – still resonate with its Celtic past.

The best way to enter Penwith is to leave St Ives in early evening and head out into the Celtic twilight along the B3306 to St Just. To the late Patrick Heron, the doyen of modern Cornish painters, this road was an essential part of the Penwith magic. 'A wonderful, enlarged footpath of a road,' he called it, 'slipping and squirming between the rocks and the fields, twisting and turning through the granite hamlets of Porthmeor and Rosemergy with a total disregard for the needs of holiday traffic.' For years it has resisted all attempts to be straightened or widened, and long may it remain as it is: one of the most dramatic drives in Britain.

Follow it west across these last few miles of England and you can feel the land running out, the sea closing in. On one side are the West Penwith moors, a pagan world of gaunt menhirs and sweeps of bracken crowned by granite outcrops twice as old as the Alps. On the other, bounded by the blue Atlantic, the low light pours across the finest prehistoric landscape in Europe, a maze of small, misshapen fields, a green-gold quilt of cattle pastures held fast since the Iron Age in a web of granite hedges.

In West Penwith the long past is everywhere. Just west of Lamorna Cove at Boleigh – the 'Field of Blood' where, according to legend, the Saxon King Athelstan crushed the last Cornish resistance – the roadsides bristle with Celtic crosses and standing stones. And a few miles on, St Buryan's church tower summons visitors to the prehistoric stone circle of Boscawen-Un.

On the edge of the moors near Sancreed I parked beside a lonely farm called Goon Vran, and walked up a narrow track to Carn Euny, the site of a farming community established two thousand years ago. Dog violets bloomed among its granite-hut circles, and stone steps led down into a fogou, a mysterious underground chamber with a roof of massive granite slabs made by the forgotten people of the moors.

Every inch of the peninsula is filled with surprises. At Madron I followed a path almost buried under a bridal veil of blackthorn blossom, to a Celtic chapel beside one of Cornwall's innumerable holy wells. Nearby, its roots clenched in the shallows of a kingcup marsh, stood the strangest sight – a goat willow covered with votive offerings. Some visitors had tied strips of coloured cloth to its branches. Others had left handkerchiefs, scarves, necklaces, ties and shoelaces. One hopeful had even left a lottery ticket. Who said tree worship was dead in Britain?

The entire landscape, with its tumbled rocks and gnarled thorn bushes flying in the wind, has the fey, eerie quality of an Arthur Rackham illustration. At Porthmeor I came upon a white goose asleep in the road. Nearby, a girl stood kissing a horse in a field, like a scene from an Irish folk tale.

But there is also a brooding sense of sadness here, a feeling of dereliction and betrayal. 'Fish, tin and copper' was a famous Cornish toast, but no more. No one will ever see the pilchard shoals spreading like cloud shadows across the sea, bringing prosperity to the fishermen of Sennen and St Ives. As for the hard-rock men of St Just, their day is done. The mines are closed, the deserted engine houses stand open to the sky, leaving only Geevor Museum at Pendeen, and the National Trust's wonderfully restored Levant beam engine on the cliffs below, to remind tourists of Penwith's industrial past.

At Sennen Cove I stayed at the Old Success Inn, named after one of the fishing companies that thrived on the mullet and pilchard shoals in earlier times. Now only tourism keeps the place alive. In one of Sennen's art and craft shops I spoke to a fisherman's wife who remembered the last time the mullet shoals swarmed in, a couple of decades ago. The occasion led to bitter rivalry between the Sennen fishermen and others from up-country. 'War was declared,' she said solemnly. 'They nearly killed each other.'

From the cliffs behind Sennen I looked down on the rock stack called the Irish Lady, her granite crinoline laced with spray, and across the bay to Land's End. Offshore, etched in black against a silver sea stood the Longships lighthouse and its sinister rocks: Carn Bras, Kettle's Bottom, the Shark's Fin and the Tal-y-maen. It is a spectacular view, but is easily upstaged by the cliff scenery higher up the Penwith coast between Cape Cornwall and Zennor Head. The wildest spot is Gurnard's Head, a forbidding, sphinx-shaped promontory exposed to the full force of the Atlantic.

In Treen Cove, in the lee of Gurnard's Head, I met a woodworker who lives in a former fisherman's cottage barely yards above the waves. So many times, he told me, dolphins play in these waters. Basking sharks cruise through the summer seas, cleaving the surface with their black angular dorsal fins, and once, back in the 1970s, he had seen a huge shoal of mullet. 'An inky shadow, solid with fish, stretching from end to end of the cove.'

Paradoxically, the wildest coast of all lies to the south of Land's End, between Penberth Cove and Pordenack Point, where gulls wail endlessly above the zawns or chasms, and the waves break with gasping force against the buttressed cliffs. In springtime the clifftops become a giant rock garden smothered in wild flowers – bluebells, alliums, primroses and violets – to be followed in early summer by foxglove spires and pincushion clumps of thrift. And nowhere is the coastal scenery more uplifting than at the fortress cliffs of Treryn Dinas, a granite headland overlooking white curves of sand.

Penberth Cove, now cared for by the National Trust, like so much of the Cornish coast, is an archetypal fishing cove: a dozen small boats hauled up on a steep stone slipway; an old wooden capstan, a clutter of crab pots, a handful of cottages and a clear stream bubbling under a clapper bridge. The cliffs may be windswept, but these seaward-running valley bottoms are almost subtropical, with their sheltered jungles of bamboos and hazel thickets.

Porthgwarra, where you can walk down to the sea through a cave, is the starting point for a glorious section of the long-distance South West Coast Path that leads past Gwennap Head towards Land's End. Out here, there is not a tree in sight; even the ubiquitous Cornish gorse bushes have been pruned to near ground level by the sea winds. In winter you could be blown off your feet, but in midsummer, when the sun is shining and the thrift is in flower and the sea is as blue as the Aegean, you would not wish to be anywhere else.

Around Pendower Cove the cliffs are seamed and fissured, forming fantastic sculpted shapes, like Easter Island statues. Ahead lies the mouth of a sea cave big enough to hide a tall ship, with Nanjizal Bay just around the corner. Another couple of miles would bring you to Land's End itself, where souvenir shops, exhibitions and the Last Labyrinth Theatre mark the most westerly point in England. But what you see between Porthgwarra and Pordenack is the real Land's End – the spiritual grand finale of the most exhilarating coastal walk in Britain.

A Passion for Peregrines

North Cornwall, March 1999

Long before I lived in Dorset, the lure of the West Country had taken hold, and not a year has passed in which I have not crossed the Tamar to revisit the Cornish coves where all my childhood holidays were spent. For me, the magic is as strong as ever, the feeling of the sea taking over, the land running out as you follow the sun.

Cornwall has the lean, spare beauty of a land long exposed to the elements. There is no fat on it. You can feel its ribs through the turf under your feet, and see where the quilted fields fall away to reveal a gaunt breastbone of granite running from Bodmin Moor all the way down to the treeless parishes of West Penwith.

It was Cornwall that taught me long ago how weather can change a landscape, what happens when a sudden sea fret comes rolling in over the hedge banks, and why so many artists come to paint the pure Atlantic sea light. Now here I was, crossing the Tamar once again, this time in twilight with a fine rain falling on Brunel's bridge. At Bodmin Road the station walls glittered black and wet in the lamplight and the night was chill, holding that indefinable smell, perhaps of the sea, not so far off, and the acid odours of the ancient moor by which I would know Cornwall with my eyes shut.

What had brought me back were the peregrines that have bred on Cornwall's Atlantic coast since time immemorial. Here is a bird that is a masterpiece of aerodynamic design, a million times more complex than any jetfighter. When it stoops, diving out of the sun towards its unsuspecting quarry, its speed can exceed two hundred miles an hour; and its lustrous lemon-rimmed eyes are eight times sharper than our own.

Everything I ever learned about these fabulous falcons I learned at the feet of Dick Treleaven, a man as Cornish as his name. In his time he had been an infantry commander, painter and falconer, but spent all his last years watching peregrines on the cliffs in fair weather and foul. For him there was no finer sight in nature than this yellow-fisted killer with the Genghis Khan moustache and harsh, heckling cry. 'Peregrines are an obsession with me,' he said. 'I love to watch them cleave the air with that immense sense of purpose. For me they are the embodiment of the wild places in which they live and have their being.'

His passion for these glorious raptors began in, of all unlikely places, London. It was in the late 1940s; he had just returned from fighting the Japanese in the Burma Campaign during World War II and was window-shopping in Piccadilly. Suddenly, a painting caught his eye. It was a portrait of a Greenland falcon by George Lodge, perhaps the finest wildlife artist of his day.

He went inside and saw more pictures, including a peregrine that captured his imagination. 'Two things happened as a result,' he explained. 'I began to paint and I returned home determined to see a wild peregrine, and discovered to my surprise that Cornwall was the best place in England for observing them.'

With his arms waving like a conductor at the last night of the Proms, eyes ablaze with a wild predatory gleam, I still remember him describing the first kill he ever saw – a hunt that ended when the tiercel (male peregrine) grabbed a pigeon directly above him. 'Feathers trickled down over my head and shoulders,' he said. 'I felt as if I had been anointed.'

In 1951 he took up falconry, the better to be able to paint hawks, joining the close-knit and eccentric brotherhood that met regularly at Hallworthy to fly their birds on Bodmin Moor. His first hawk was a goshawk called Crasher that he used to carry around Bude on his fist. 'One day I overheard these two kids talking as I went past,' he told me. "There he goes," said one to the other, "old Plus-Fours and his bloody sparrow."'

Crasher was followed by a succession of other hawks, including a lanner falcon from Benghazi and another goshawk called Sammy Snatchit who escaped and was last seen perched on a railway signal in Basingstoke. But he never kept a peregrine. 'They owe allegiance to nobody,' he declared. 'I know the peregrine is the falconer's dream, but I could never own one. It is too noble a bird to be captive. It has to be free. It belongs high on a clifftop, and that is where I like to see it fly and hear it scream.'

Sadly, Dick died in 2009, but not before he had been awarded the MBE in recognition of his lifelong dedication to the birds whose behaviour he knew better than anyone before or since.

Dick Treleaven it was who had shown me the way to the coast, down a narrow lane between squat hedge banks of Delabole slate, built Cornish style in herringbone patterns, from whose crevices the fleshy leaves of pennywort erupted like green blisters. Where the lane ended on the open cliffs the ferocity of the winter gales had torn at the bracken until only the wiry main stems remained. Yet even here, among the most sheltered tussocks and in south-facing hollows out of the wind, early primroses told of returning spring.

The day was cheerless but the coast was alive with birds. Herring gulls hung in the up-draughts, crook-winged, wailing, rising and falling about the pillars and buttresses of yawning chasms. Somewhere a raven grunted beneath an overhang. Fulmars gabbled as they planed over the swell and boomeranged around the cove before landing on guano-spattered crags, and above the mumble of the sea arose the fretful piping of oystercatchers and the deeper, menacing bark of a marauding black-backed gull.

The wind was raw and I cast around the lichen-scabbed rocks and coconut-scented gorse thickets for a place to shelter and scan the black cliff on the far side of the cove, looking for the resident pair of peregrine falcons whose eyrie was hidden at the back of a grassy ledge halfway up the rock face.

Even before I found them I could hear them screaming, and suddenly there they were, both birds together, flickering in from the sea. Almost at once the female (known simply as the falcon) disappeared behind the headland, but I watched the tiercel land on a cushion of thrift and begin to tug at something anchored firmly beneath his yellow feet. Grey feathers floated away on the wind and I realised I had just missed a kill. Most likely it was the falcon that had made the kill and had brought in the pigeon for her mate, who was now greedily tearing red hunks of meat from the plumed carcass.

During the winter the falcon is the dominant hunter. She it is who makes most of the kills, virtually feeding the smaller tiercel. In winter, too, these Cornish peregrines range further afield, wandering inland on their hunting forays, but still returning to roost on the coast.

On another part of the cliff a pair of ravens had lodged their nest of sticks in a narrow rock chimney. Their breeding season had begun even before that of the peregrines. For weeks the female had been sitting on a clutch of freckled sea-green eggs. Now, although there were newly hatched chicks in the nest, both parents spent more time in the air, tumbling and flying in perfect unison, wingtip to wingtip, feet dangling. Sometimes one bird would peel away in a long, looping dive, only to rejoin its mate moments later, their black pinions almost touching, like outstretched fingers.

It was now nearly noon, time for lunch. I dug into my backpack, unwrapped a pasty and poured coffee into a plastic mug that I cupped with both hands to thaw my frozen fingers. At that moment, just as I was about to raise the mug to my lips there was a sudden commotion and every gull and jackdaw on the cliff was aloft, wheeling and crying.

I did not take long to find out the reason for the commotion. Halfway down the cliff the two ravens had cornered a buzzard on a ledge near their nest. The buzzard was clearly unhappy and mewed plaintively as it sought to defend itself; but the ravens were merciless. Their throats swelled, their hackles rose and their guttural barks rang around the cove as they chased the buzzard from ledge to ledge.

At times it seemed as if they were deliberately baiting their victim. While one raven shuffled forward, croaking loudly, its mate would sneak up behind and tweak the buzzard by the tail. Once they almost forced it into the sea; but at last it managed to gain height and flap ignominiously to safety, mobbed by gulls until finally it took refuge in a hedge. Meanwhile the ravens, having tired of their sport, were performing a victory roll over the cliffs. High overhead the bold buccaneers twirled and tumbled. Their jet-black plumage shone with glossy green and purple glints as they rolled in a single shaft of sunlight and finally disappeared beyond the headland.

So intent had I been on watching the ravens that I never saw the falcon return to her favourite hunting perch high up under the lip of the cliff. One minute there was nothing but bare rock; the next she was there, alert and upright, a furious gargoyle glaring out to sea.

Her sudden appearance is typical of the peregrine. How swift it is, how mysterious its secret comings and goings; assured and complete, it belongs to a world more ancient than our own, moved by visions we can only guess at, living a freedom we can never know.

By now the sun had broken through, although the sea wind was as cold as ever, and both the falcon and the tiercel were aloft. Even through my binoculars they were mere specks, yet they seemed to dominate the landscape beneath. At first it appeared they were simply revelling in the joy of flight, carving immense parabolas across the sky and almost playing with the pigeons that scattered in panic at every leisurely stoop. And still I waited.

Afternoon came. The wind dropped. The sun became warmer and a big mottled seal appeared at the base of the cliffs, bobbing like a bottle in the cove's green depths.

Winter or summer, the magic of this savage coast never fails. On either side the cliffs fall sheer, sometimes breaking away to form barnacled reefs, dark islands and towers of bristling rock at whose feet the heaving swell booms and subsides with sinister gasps.

Above me the falcon was back at her pitch. She has evolved a method of hunting that is entirely suited to the lie of the land and the predictable movements of the pigeons that are her favourite prey. When she leaves the cliff she flies like a fugitive, dropping swiftly towards the sea to disappear behind the headland. There she lets the up-blast lift her, riding with it until she is in view once more.

Inland, gulls are circling in a thermal and she glides towards them, ringing up on the warm currents of air until she is no more than a black star blinking among the crests and summits of the towering clouds. Now she drifts, going towards the sun, following the line of the coast for perhaps a mile, to the inlet where the pigeons breed. She has learned the ways of pigeons, which leave the cliffs every day and pass up the shallow valley to feed in the fields.

From her lofty ambush among the clouds, nothing escapes her binocular vision: white specks of gulls glancing over the ploughland; black rooks and grapeshot bursts of starlings; but what she is looking for is the piebald flicker of feral pigeons and at once she accelerates. Her bow-bent wings beat faster, so fast that I can almost sense the hunger burning inside her, driving her forward with an unmistakable sense of purpose.

Unable to take my eyes off her in case I lose her, I cannot yet see what she can see, but I know that she is hunting, and I remember something Dick Treleaven once told me: 'Peregrines don't really *chase* pigeons,' he said. 'Their whole strategy is based on interception.' And it's true. Somewhere beneath her, as yet unaware of danger, a flock of pigeons is heading for home.

From a mile high the falcon tips forward, folds her wings and stoops, faster than a falling stone. Her dive carries her below the skyline, where she is harder to see against the dun colours of the moor; but now for the first time I pick up her quarry. The pigeons scatter as she swoops beneath them and then bounds up to snatch at a straggler. She misses – levels out over Hendra, skimming over the bare fields with white gulls boiling in her wake. On she goes, streaking low over the stone walls, past squat church towers and farms slate-roofed against the gales – and misses again.

But she is not done yet. Now she rings up, turns and flies directly towards us, passing overhead in an effortless glide, her wings dark blades, yellow feet bunched up behind. I can see her round head swivelling and briefly feel her gaze upon me as she scans the ground beneath, and as she swings out over the cliffs the sun outlines her body in a wash of burning gold. Once more she climbs: the cloud biter, the beautiful barbarian, 'waiting on at her pitch' in the words of the old falconers, a thousand feet above the headland.

Then comes another searing stoop, corkscrewing down towards her target; and this time her dive takes her right into the cove, whipping low over the waves as if intent on committing suicide by smashing into the cliffs; but at the last moment she bounds upwards almost vertically to alight on a buttress near the eyrie. Grey feathers drift away from the motionless shadow beneath her feet and her triumphant scream floats back across the abyss.

Stargazing in Stag Country

Exmoor National Park, October 2012

On Winsford Hill the darkness is absolute. There is no moon, no light of any kind except for the distant galaxy of the Welsh coast glittering with frosty brilliance on the eastern horizon, and a few remote farmsteads blinking like red dwarfs in the unseen combes below. Otherwise, Exmoor is one vast black hole of silence – the perfect venue for a spot of stargazing.

Exmoor National Park is one of the few corners of England where low levels of light pollution allow visitors to enjoy night skies that have long since disappeared elsewhere, and last autumn it was designated as an International Dark Sky Reserve – the first place in Europe to receive this accolade.

'In London you can only see about two hundred stars,' says Simon Ould, a science teacher and Fellow of the Royal Astronomical Society who tours the Southwest with his own mobile planetarium. 'On Exmoor you can see thousands.' And it's true. From end to end the heavens are ablaze with their cold fire. Ould has brought a telescope with him, powerful enough to observe the rings of Jupiter and its four moons; but I prefer just to stand and stare as he points out the most prominent stars.

The constellation of the Plough – referred to in the Bible as the Seven Stars and in Homer's *Iliad* as the Bear – is instantly recognisable. So is Orion the Hunter, cartwheeling over the Brendon Hills with Sirius the Dog Star at his heels. Others are less familiar, and Ould directs my gaze to where the constellation of Cygnus, the Swan, is diving through the Milky Way. 'The light from Deneb, the star that marks the Swan's tail, was emitted when Iron Age farmers lived on Exmoor,' he says. 'As for the Milky Way itself, even if we could travel at the speed of light it would still take a hundred thousand years to cross.'

In Dulverton next morning the clear skies have vanished, and the Barle Valley with its salmon pools and hanging woods is gift-wrapped in fog when I set out to look for the wild red deer that have lived on Exmoor since prehistoric times. Despite the poor visibility there is still a good chance of seeing them, because my guide is Richard Eales, a national park ranger with a passion for red deer. 'We have about four thousand living here,' he tells me as we set off in his mud-spattered Land Rover. 'That's half of all the red deer in England.'

It's the stags I really want to see – Britain's largest wild land mammals. On reaching maturity at seven years old these monarchs of the combes with their hat-rack antlers can tip the scales at three hundred pounds, and during the October rut the hillsides echo to their guttural bellowing – known as 'bolving' on Exmoor.

For the past nine years the rutting season has coincided with what is surely Britain's weirdest stag night, when contestants gather in the hills above Dulverton to compete for the title of Exmoor Bolving Champion. People come from miles around and the competitors cup their hands and roar like a lovelorn stag in the hope of getting a response from the real thing. 'The idea was dreamed up over a pint at the Rock Inn in Dulverton,' says Eales, and he should know. He is the reigning champion.

Now it is midwinter. The rut is long past and deer are not so easy to find. We drive up onto the roof of the moor, where the River Exe is born in a desolation of rushes and quaking mires, but see nothing except a pair of ravens. With mist as thick as sheep's wool in Long Chains Combe we return to the road south of Brendon Two Gates and look down into Prayway Meads where the infant Exe – still no wider than a ditch – dribbles down a deep cleft in the hillside.

The sombre colours of the moor in winter make spotting difficult as we scan the slopes with binoculars. But eventually patience is rewarded by the sight of a big stag watching us from half a mile off in the heather. 'Nice one,' says Eales with a contented grin. 'All his rights and three atop,' meaning the antlers are fully developed, complete with brow, bay and trey tines, plus three points on each side. Later during my stay I will see whole herds of deer on the slopes of Dunkery near Webbers Post, but nothing to match the thrill of my first Exmoor stag.

Although deer are Eales' speciality, he also seems to be on first-name terms with the Exmoor ponies. 'That's Dave,' he says, pointing to a shaggy little stallion in the roadside bracken. With their mealy muzzles and small ears these British hill ponies belong to a hardy breed whose lineage goes back to Celtic times. Although there are about 3,500 worldwide, only 350 roam free on Exmoor itself, where they can survive the harshest conditions. In winter they eat gorse and heather and are so perfectly insulated against the cold that snow can settle on their backs without melting.

It is hard to get under the skin of Exmoor, but after a few days I am hooked for life. Unlike Dartmoor, whose rugged good looks are built of granite, its smooth, bare skylines reveal the West Country's more feminine side; and although Exmoor is one of Britain's smallest parks, its 267 square miles are crammed full of marvels, from Tarr Steps, the medieval stone clapper bridge spanning the Barle, to the coast between Porlock and Lynmouth, where giant hog-backed hills plunge headlong for a thousand feet into the Bristol Channel – the highest cliffs in England. One moment you find yourself up in the clouds among the standing stones and heathery sweeps of open moorland. Then suddenly you are swooping down sunken lanes full of suicidal pheasants, past tumbling streams and medieval farmsteads lost in the hush of the enfolding combes. In the holiday season these backcountry byways with their bottom-gear hills and hairpin bends must be tricky to negotiate; but in winter you can have them all to yourself.

The pheasants are a reminder of how field sports still underpin the Exmoor economy, as they have done since the days when tweed-clad industrialists such as the Colmans of Norwich would turn up in their mustard-yellow Rolls-Royce for a spot of shooting. Nowadays, of course, it is tourism that is in the driving seat, and adding a dash of romance to it all is the story of *Lorna Doone*.

Set in the time of the Monmouth Rebellion, R. D. Blackmore's novel was inspired by tales of the Dounes, a notorious band of Scottish brigands who settled on Exmoor in the seventeenth century. The book was published in 1869, and by the 1920s readers were flocking to what would soon become known as Lorna Doone Country – a godsend to the tourist trade.

'Blackmore dramatised his story to such an extent that he made Badgworthy Water sound more like Glencoe,' says Rob Wilson-North, the park's resident landscape archaeologist and an expert on the history of Lorna Doone's Exmoor. 'It's a fictionalised landscape.

If you tried to follow it with a map as some readers do you would soon be completely lost.' Even so, visitors are still drawn to Malmsmead on Badgworthy Water, and the church at Oare with its lime-washed porch, where Carver Doone shot Lorna on her wedding day.

'What fascinates me about Exmoor,' says Wilson-North, 'is the impact of all the people who have lived here, from the Mesolithic hunter-gatherers to Coleridge and Wordsworth and right up to the present day.'

As if to underline the point we stop at Porlock Stone Circle, a moorland monument believed to have been laid out by its megalithic builders in response to celestial observation – proof positive that even in those far-off times Exmoor's starlit skies were a source of endless wonder.

The Exe Factor

Dawlish Warren, Devon, December 2010

Locked in the bone-clenching midwinter chill, Devon lies silent under a pewter sky. At Dawlish Warren the beach is deserted, but inland the Exe estuary is bursting with life. At this time of year it is hard to imagine the South Devon coast as England's Riviera, but there is no better season in which to discover the secret world of the Exe.

Born in a bog near Simonsbath, the Exe is a contrary river. From its modest beginnings on the roof of Exmoor it is only five miles to the Bristol Channel. But, perversely, it strikes out in the opposite direction, heading for the English Channel sixty miles away. At first it flows swiftly, hurrying between steep-wooded hillsides, but at Tiverton it develops a middle-aged spread and becomes a gentler river as it meanders down to Exeter. And it is here, just south of the M5 motorway, that the estuary begins.

Six miles long by a mile across at its widest point, the estuary finally meets the sea at Exmouth, the southernmost point of the Jurassic Coast World Heritage Site. From end to end it is a Site of Special Scientific Interest and it is also a Ramsar site, a global designation putting it in the same league as the Florida Everglades and the Camargue. Its mudflats and sandbanks are as rich as a rainforest, stuffed full with worms, clams and tiny snails, thick as currants in a Christmas pudding – and this is the Exe factor that makes it a major refuge for wintering wildfowl.

'A cubic metre of estuary mud contains the same calorific value as fourteen Mars Bars,' says Sally Mills, the local RSPB reserves' warden. 'And that's what pulls in the birds.'

Until a few months ago Sally was warden on Aride Island in the Seychelles. Now, despite the difference in temperature, she is equally passionate about the Exe. So much so that she has even commandeered the Topsham Turf Ferry to take me on a half-day cruise.

With the tide falling fast we hurry down to Trout's Boatyard in Topsham, where the blue-and-white-painted *Sea Dream II* is moored at the quayside. Steve Garratt, her skipper, is an ex-Royal Navy helicopter pilot who retired to live here five years ago. That was when he bought *Sea Dream II*. 'She was built on the beach at Teignmouth eighty years ago and is still going strong,' he says proudly. Today, as well as ferrying people to the Turf Hotel in the main holiday season, he also operates winter birding cruises for the RSPB.

Now, with Garratt at the wheel, we go with the flow, puttering downstream into an opalescent morning haze, following the main channel as it hugs the mudflats of Greenland Bank. In this no-man's land between the tides, everything is agleam: the shining water; the glittering flats. The mist has completely erased the horizon, making it impossible to tell where sea ends and sky begins, and wherever I look there are birds.

Curlews stalk purposefully along the shoreline. Feeding parties of avocets create a black and white ballet as they scythe the shallows with up-curved bills. Flocks of godwits hurtle past on flickering wings. Dunlin – another name for them is sea mice – scurry among stranded clumps of bladderwrack, and chevrons of brent geese fly overhead on their way to graze on Exminster Marshes.

These brents are the dark-bellied race that comes from Arctic Russia; up to 1,500 of them spend the winter here, says Sally Mills, 'and we can tell by the numbers of young birds that arrive if it has been a good or bad lemming year in the Arctic. When lemmings are plentiful the Arctic foxes and other predators have lots to eat and spare the goslings. But a bad lemming year is bad news for the geese, and this winter we haven't seen many juveniles.'

Midway down the estuary between Powderham and Lympstone we turn and head for Turf Lock at the entrance to the Exeter Ship Canal. There is nobody else around. The yachts moored three abreast in the canal are battened down for winter and the slate-hung Turf Hotel is closed.

We follow the towpath past Exminster Marshes. Gulls scream in the windless air, and the estuary is like a mirror, grey and muted under thickening cloud, a monochrome world relieved only by the lion-coloured walls of canal-side reeds. 'The estuary is always changing,' says Sally Mills. 'It's never the same from one hour to the next.'

Back in Topsham there is still time to explore before nightfall. I stroll down the Strand, a Millionaire's Row of Dutch-gabled houses overlooking the water. At the far end is the Goat Walk, a path beside the sea wall that eventually turns inland to Bowling Green Marshes, where snipe fly up from ice-rimmed pools.

Next day, revived by a cosy night at the Globe Hotel, I move on to Dawlish Warren at the estuary mouth. The Warren is a giant sandbar stretching towards Exmouth for a mile and a half. On its seaward side runs a line of sand hills bristling with marram grass, and the land behind it is a National Nature Reserve, a wilderness of rabbit-cropped turf with a golf course in the middle of it.

With my binoculars I can see hundreds of oystercatchers on the sandbar known as Bull Hill. They come every day to feed on the mussel beds, hammering open the shells with their coral-red bills until the tide drives them off.

Come lunchtime and I'm feeling peckish, too. So it's off to the Anchor at Cockwood, a mile up the estuary. 'Cock'ood', as the locals call it, would not be the same without its seventeenth-century harbour-side inn. Originally a seaman's mission, it boasts open fires, beams galore and even a friendly ghost and his dog. But best of all is its seafood menu, offering mussels, fresh daily from the Exe and cooked in thirty different ways.

Afterwards I return to the Warren for a last look at the sea. In summer the dunes are overrun, but in winter this is a lonely spot, shriven by the wind, reclaimed by the wild, and when at last the sun goes down the sky is filled with skeins of duck.

Driving home past Powderham Castle I can see fallow deer grazing under parkland oaks. Their antlered heads stare from the shadows. At Exeter it is almost dark, and out in the estuary the oystercatchers will be feeding again, falling on Bull Hill in shrilling droves until the tide drives them back once more.

Lost in Scrumpy Land

Avalon Marshes, Somerset, January 2014

G oing west with the sun down the A303 from Wincanton there is no hint of what lies just beyond the highway. But peel off through Martock and in minutes you'll find you have swapped the fast lane for a bygone cheese-and-scrumpy world in which eel-catchers and basket-weavers still make a living and life moves at a different pace. Uneven roads that ripple with subsidence lead you down raised causeways lined with pollard willows, past hedgerow trees festooned with mistletoe and Hamstone villages with solemn church towers that beckon across the low-lying fields.

Into this land of the seven rivers – Axe, Brue, Cary, Isle, Tone, Parrett and Yeo – pours the runoff from the surrounding hills. The result is more East Anglia than West Country: a chequerboard of comely fields weighed down by fat cattle, its spongy pastures crosshatched by brimming dykes and ditches. Welcome to the Levels – the vast Somerset fenland that stretches across 150,000 acres of waterlogged countryside from Taunton to the Mendips.

Here, all it takes is a turn of the wheel to find oneself lost in a timeless landscape where the sense of the past is palpable. At Shapwick Heath National Nature Reserve you can see where the oldest path in Britain was unearthed. Here ran the Sweet Track, a Neolithic boardwalk, traversing Somerset's peat-bog jungles six thousand years ago. In places the peat is thirty feet deep. Some spots are nearly twenty feet below the high-tide mark in Bridgwater Bay and much of the land is so low-lying that vast areas are thought to have been overwhelmed in 1607 by a tsunami.

Across the flatness of the Levels, distant landmarks draw the eye, and none more so than the enigmatic hilltop called Glastonbury Tor. Approach it from any direction and you can see why, in Somerset, all ley lines lead to Glastonbury. Capped by the beckoning finger of St Michael's Tower, it dominates the view for miles.

For centuries this enigmatic hilltop has wrapped itself in a fantasy world of Dark Age myths from which it is impossible to extract the truth. Suffice to say, they involve Joseph of Arimathea and the Chalice of the Last Supper, a Holy Thorn that blooms at Christmas and the last resting-place of King Arthur and Guinevere in Glastonbury Abbey ruins.

It was the Saxons who gave Somerset its name, thought to mean the land of the summer farm-dwellers; but it is in winter that the Levels come into their own. Sometimes it brings great floods, as in 1929, when bread was handed up on hayforks to families marooned in upstairs rooms; in our own time, in 2014, there was a repeat in which the inhabitants of Muchelney – the 'Large Isle' of King Alfred's England – were cut off for almost a fortnight.

To the west of Glastonbury lie the Avalon Marshes – a sprawling flatness of meres and reed beds, old peat workings and cattle pasture locked in a framework of sword-straight dykes, known locally as rhynes and pronounced 'reens'. For the RSPB this is one of Britain's most precious wetland habitats. Here every evening at Ham Wall and Shapwick Heath millions of starlings – mostly migrants from Scandinavia – fly in to roost, swirling overhead in shape-shifting clouds as if orchestrated by a single voice. As a wildlife spectacle this midwinter matinee is right up there with the greatest and is now so popular that the RSPB has even installed a starling hotline to advise visitors where best to see them.

Otters and bitterns share the starlings' winter refuge, and elsewhere, in the outlying fields around Alfred's old guerrilla stronghold at Athelney, you might be lucky enough to spot a flock of cranes – a species lost to Britain for four hundred years but now being reintroduced to the Levels. With their angle-poise legs and forlorn bugling voices there's something magical about these grey ghosts of the wetlands, as if they had stepped from the pages of an East European fairy tale.

By the time the snowdrops are blooming in East Lambrook Manor Garden, the starlings are returning to their breeding haunts; but by then an altogether stealthier migrant is arriving by the million.

The coming of the elvers, the eel's multitudinous offspring, marks the end of an epic three-thousand-mile journey from their spawning grounds in the Sargasso Sea. They reach Somerset as 'glass eels', matchstick-thin with transparent bodies, swarming up the River Parrett to seek the ponds, streams and ditches where they will grow into adults – and the unlucky ones will end up in the Brown and Forrest Smokery at Hambridge.

As a local delicacy, smoked eel takes some beating and is as much a part of Somerset as Cheddar cheese or the cider made just down the road under Burrow Hill. Here, surrounded by a sea of orchards, is Burrow Hill Farm, the home of Julian Temperley, cider-maker extraordinary, prophet of the Slow Food Movement and a passionate believer in the French concept of *terroir* – the importance of local produce.

No one knows how long the apple tree has blossomed in Britain; but while southern Europe has embraced the vine, Somerset's rich soil and our damp English climate have conspired to make cider the *grand cru* of the West Country.

Temperley started in 1968 with twenty-seven acres and now has 170 acres planted with apple trees. Stand in their midst and you see nothing but colonnades of bare trunks, row on row, a cider cathedral with a fan vaulting of branches that meet overhead and shut out the sky.

In his farmhouse kitchen Temperley shows me his bible – two volumes of the *Herefordshire Pomona*. Published in the 1870s and '80s, they are illustrated with exquisite colour plates of classic cider apples such as Foxwhelp, Scarlet Nonpareil and the bitter-sharp Kingston Black.

Across the yard in his ciderhouse the air smells damp and sweet as sin. Reverently I tiptoe past a row of giant wooden butts slumbering in the shadows. Put an ear to their cavernous paunches when the cider is fermenting, the cider-makers of yesteryear used to say, and you could hear them sing. 'We still look at ourselves as local farm cider-makers,' says Temperley, 'and the art of blending the apple varieties is what our cider-making is all about.'

But cider brandy is what he is best known for, having resurrected a process that has been around in this country for nearly four hundred years, and at the far end of the ciderhouse are two elderly French calvados stills he bought in Normandy in the 1990s. Fifi and Josephine, he calls them, and both play their part in the mysterious alchemy that transforms crushed apples into the precious liquid which, after ageing in oak barrels, emerges as clear and golden as distilled sunlight.

Matured for up to twenty years, Temperley's Somerset cider brandies now grace some of the finest tables in the land. One of the most popular is Shipwreck, distilled in 1999 and kept in oak barrels retrieved from the wreck of the *Napoli* on the East Devon coast in 2007. 'Someone ought to make a film about it,' says Temperley. 'It's our Somerset version of *Whisky Galore*.'

Red Kite Country

Tregaron, Ceredigion, January 1985

Cors Caron is a sombre place. Its colours are the muted shades of winter reeds and tussock sedge, a waste of willow carr and heather relieved only by the treacherous green of sphagnum beds, and sometimes by the thinner branches of the birch trees that in certain lights glow like port wine.

There was no shelter from the wind. The hills of mid-Wales lay along the horizon, dull as bruises. A raven sat on a fence post, waiting for something to die, and far out in the emptiness of the bog, under a sky heavy with the threat of snow, shaggy ponies were grazing at the edge of a thicket, looking for all the world like the prehistoric horses of Neolithic Britain. With fingers frozen inside two pairs of gloves I scanned the far side of the bog through binoculars and picked up a herd of twelve whooper swans sailing on a gleam of water. Nothing else moved.

Some twenty thousand years ago, the tongue of an Ice Age glacier scoured this wide basin in the Welsh hills. Later, as Britain grew warmer and the ice retreated, a boulder moraine blocked the valley, causing a shallow lake to form; and in time, when the lake silted up, Cors Caron – the Great Bog of Tregaron – was born.

Cors Caron is a perfect example of a raised mire – a type of bog that is fast disappearing from lowland Britain. Its vital ingredient is sphagnum moss, a botanical sponge so successful at mopping up water and nutrients that it forms giant carpets which create their own acid environment and in time transform the original fen into true bog.

As the mosses die they sink to the bottom, forming a thick under-carpet of peat that eventually causes the bog to rise above the surrounding land. Yet instead of drying out and draining away, the raised bog continues to grow, swelling with every winter's rains and constantly laying down peat, until after seven thousand years its domed surface may have risen up to thirty feet above the original lake bed.

Legend has it that beneath Cors Caron sleeps a buried city called Maesllyn. If so, it has never given up its secrets. Yet the bog itself has been generous for centuries, providing peat for hearth fires, dry rushes for stable bedding and grazing for livestock. The peat was cut in early summer and then stacked to dry until early autumn, when it was hauled out by horse and cart before rising water levels made the tracks impassable.

Peat cutting had ceased by 1960. Wintering snipe and teal now haunt the flooded diggings, and the Great Bog of Tregaron is a National Nature Reserve. Willow carr has invaded the wettest hollows and spread along the lowest depression known as the lagg, which encircles the bog. Here, too, are rushes and reed-canary grass and other water-loving plants, including the rotted hulks of wild iris; but as the mires rise and become more acid, cotton-grass and purple moor-grass appear, and are in turn replaced by deer grass, heather and bog rosemary, tussock sedge and heaving peat hummocks, with scatterings of gnarled birch on the drier ridges.

There are otters in the valley, for the River Teifi flows through the middle of the bog and is full of eels, as well as the migrant salmon and trout that move upstream to spawn each year. Cors Caron is also a stronghold for polecats, which prowl among its reeds and tussocks, preying on voles and sniffing out nests of snipe and redshank. Other birds that breed here in summer are mallard, curlew, reed bunting and even a few grouse. Throughout the year, buzzards, sparrowhawks, red kites and barn owls patrol the reserve – joined in winter by hen harriers, short-eared owls, peregrines and merlins.

Once it was possible to watch birds from the railway that linked Tregaron to Lampeter, with Aberystwyth to the north and Carmarthen to the south. Where the line crossed the bog it floated on a raft of wooden faggots and bales of wool. But in December 1963 heavy floods breached the track and it was never repaired. Since then the line has been taken up and the track is now a footpath for visitors to the reserve, skirting Allt-ddu Farm until after about a mile it leads to an observation tower by the Afon Fflur.

My guide and companion on this bitterly cold day was Roger Lovegrove, who gave up his career as a physical education teacher to work for the RSPB, becoming one of their most steadfast guardians, watching over the welfare of the birds of Wales from the RSPB regional headquarters at Newtown in Powys. A tall, lean man, his face furrowed by long days out of doors, he bubbles with energy, eloquence and enthusiasm, and his knowledge of wild Wales and its birds is unsurpassed. He knows every inch of the country, from the oaks of Gwenffrwd, where redstarts and pied flycatchers breed, to the winter kite roosts and lonely upland hunting grounds of the last Welsh merlins.

The tower shook in the wind as we climbed inside the hide and looked out across the valley. Someone was shooting in the fields on the other side, and the sound reverberated over the bog, sending up flights of mallard and a pair of fast-moving smaller duck that Lovegrove at once identified as teal.

We scanned the skyline with our binoculars, hoping to pick up a merlin, but in vain. We checked each distant stump and fence post, looking for short-eared owls, but found none. Then Lovegrove's sharp eyes spotted a flicker of movement low over the willow carr. I swung my glasses to where he was pointing, and as the circle of distance swam into focus I found a hen harrier, a beautiful ring-tailed female sailing on her long wings among the stunted trees.

Suddenly a swifter shape shot into view, causing the harrier to rise sharply in alarm. 'Peregrine,' whispered Lovegrove excitedly. Even at so great a distance I could make out the hawk's barbaric mask as it chased the much larger harrier into the sky. The peregrine appeared to be playing, revelling in its supreme mastery of the air, whereas the harrier – so elegant and effortless when we had first seen her – was now made to seem clumsy by comparison as she struggled to avoid its sudden stoops.

'He's pulling his punches,' grinned Lovegrove; and, sure enough, the peregrine peeled away as if tiring of its sport and began to ring up until it was a mere black star high under the racing snow clouds. Then its wings closed and it slid down the sky until its stoop became a monumental fall to earth, a dark wedge flinging downwards too fast to follow. I lost it against a blur of hills and could only guess at its whereabouts by the shrapnel bursts of panic-stricken lapwings that blew up in its wake across the distant fields.

A peregrine aloft is like no other bird. It carries with it a constant aura of imminent drama, and so long as it remains in the air it possesses this extraordinary power to dominate the horizons. So it was at Tregaron; and when the peregrine had gone, the bog fell silent again, waiting for the snow that had threatened all morning and was sure to come soon.

Nor did the harrier return, so we walked back to the car and tried to thaw out with a flask of hot coffee and sandwiches. Then we left Cors Caron and headed north through Pontrhydfendigaid and Pontrhydygroes, following the River Ystwyth into one of the loveliest valleys in mid-Wales. We passed Hafod church and at last came to a high lane among lonely hills with thick woods of oak and larch reaching towards us, and the Ystwyth writhing in silver coils through the meadows below.

Squalls of hail swept the hills – to be followed by a strange, granular snow that dusted the summits and settled like hoar frost in the lane. We parked in a lay-by looking down into the vertiginous valley and waited for the red kites Lovegrove knew would soon come drifting in to roost in the oaks below us.

The return of the red kite is a resounding success story for British wildlife conservation, and for the RSPB in particular. It was not always a rare bird. In Elizabethan times red kites were regular scavengers in the streets of London, and they remained common until the late eighteenth century. But then followed the age of intensive game preservation in which all predators were regarded as vermin, to be killed by any means. Easy to shoot, even simpler to poison, the red kite never stood a chance. By 1870 it had gone from England. Thirty years later the last Scottish red kites had been wiped out, leaving the hills of central Wales as the bird's last refuge. Here at the turn of the century a handful of pairs survived among the remote and unkeepered valleys, and clung on long enough for more enlightened views to prevail.

In the 1930s, the lowest point in the red kite's history, they were down to their last ten pairs, and for two decades they hovered at the edge of the abyss. How close did they come to disappearing altogether? 'About as close as you can get,' says Lovegrove. 'Scientists established that in 1931 there was only one successful breeding female. The entire Welsh kite population up to the 1970s was descended from that single hen.'

Since then, aided by round-the-clock protection at nest sites in the breeding season, the red kite has clawed its way back from the brink, and has become a red badge of courage for a region where resilience in the face of adversity is almost a way of life.

'In Wales nobody has a bad word to say about the red kite,' says Lovegrove. 'Everyone knows they are totally incapable of killing a lamb. They have no substance to them. They are as light as thistledown, and even when they find a carcass they must wait for the ravens to make the first inroads.'

Their recovery has been painfully slow, but today the red kite is no longer the rarest breeding bird of prey in Wales; that dubious privilege has passed to the merlin. Yet the red kite still breeds only in Wales[2] and its presence here is the motivating spark that gives these hills their tension.

Red kites are among our biggest birds of prey, with a wingspan well over five feet; yet they weigh less than a buzzard. The reason lies in their lifestyle. Kites are true lords of the air, designed to soar for long periods over the hills and valleys in search of carrion.

In kite country there is always a tingling sense of anticipation. The eye scours the hilltops, yearning for a glimpse of that rakish

---

[2] Since then the red kite has continued its remarkable comeback and continues to extend its range. Like the red gold once mined in these hills by the Romans, kites have become a precious local resource, attracting tourists from far beyond Wales. Rescued from virtual extinction by one of the world's longest-running protection programmes, the species has been successfully reintroduced to many parts of England and Scotland and, more recently, to Northern Ireland. Today's UK population of red kites is around 1,800 breeding pairs (about seven per cent of the world population).

silhouette, the long wings bent against the pluck of the wind, and a fanned fork tail – the kite's true trademark – deep-etched against a winter sky.

Now, singly and in pairs, the first birds began to arrive, sailing and circling over the head of the valley. By day they hunt alone or in pairs, scavenging over the hills for dead sheep or rabbits, sometimes travelling up to fifteen miles but always returning to their communal winter roosts among the sheltering oaks. At one point I spotted six red kites in view at the same time. Later I counted nine spiralling together.

They flew in the teeth of the wind, heedless of the slanting snow that reduced the more distant birds to wraiths. Some passed within fifty feet of where we sat, and one came so close that I could see every detail of its plumage, as if in a measured drawing. Its body and wing coverts were brown and tawny like November oaks. The red tail drew its colour from the dead bracken, and the head and wing patches were as one with the hills under their dusting of snow. And still they came, rocking and swaying on crooked wings, riding in on the blizzard as dusk began to fall around us. By the time we left we had counted at least thirty: one quarter of all the red kites of Wales. Even Lovegrove was thrilled. 'In twenty years of birdwatching in Wales, that is the most I have seen in a single day,' he said.

The Island of the Tides

Bardsey, Gwynedd, August 2014

High summer in North Wales, and holidaymakers are not the only visitors to the Llyn Peninsula. On Bardsey Island thousands of Manx shearwaters fill the night skies with their unearthly caterwauling as they return to breed in their cliffside burrows; and on the Gwylan Islands off Aberdaron, hundreds of puffins are busily feeding their chicks.

Seabirds are only part of the magic that clings to this special corner of the Principality. Follow the coastal footpath from Aberdaron and the farther you travel the stronger becomes the feeling of the land running out, leaving the rest of Britain far behind. Below the path lies a succession of sandy coves and beaches, each one sheltered by haggard headlands and lapped by an emerald sea so clear it could be the Mediterranean. But this is the Llyn Peninsula, the Land's End of North Wales, a tapering finger of patchwork fields and brooding hilltops separating Caernarfon Bay from Tremadoc Bay.

The final stretch is crisscrossed by lanes barely wide enough for a car, many leading to nowhere but lonely farmhouses high above the sea, until at last you are standing on the cliffs at Braich-y-Pwll, with nothing between you and the blue horizon but the whale-backed silhouette of Bardsey Island.

The comparisons with Cornwall are everywhere: in the dolmens and standing stones, the Dark Age saints and holy wells, the smell of the bracken and the crying gulls. But there the likeness ends and Llyn's empty beaches are a revelation. Among the loveliest are the famous whistling sands of Porth Oer, a bathing cove on the north coast. At every step they squeak underfoot like a startled kitten; and when I was there on a sunny morning in peak season I counted no more than a dozen families. Had it been Polzeath or Newquay the beach would have been packed from end to end.

Looking back up the peninsula from the National Trust viewpoint at Carreg, above Porth Oer, what you see is a dragon's spine of volcanic summits receding through broken light and shadow towards the dim outlines of Snowdonia. Llyn's loftiest point is Yr Eifl, 1,841 feet high, with an Iron Age fort on its flanks and breathtaking views of Anglesey, the immense arc of Cardigan Bay and even the Wicklow Mountains on a clear day.

The National Trust's familiar oak-leaf symbol is everywhere, not only in the gardens of Plas y Rhiw above Cardigan Bay but also at its new Porth y Swnt interpretation centre in Aberdaron and along the thirty miles of coastline it has acquired over the years, including most of the dramatic cliffs and headlands looking out to Bardsey at the very toe end of the Peninsula.

Having clocked up a number of islands around the British Isles over the years – Lundy, Bryher, Fair Isle, the Skelligs – I was desperate to add Bardsey to the list. And so, on a perfect cloudless morning, I walked down the narrow valley that leads to Porth Meudwy, the lobster fishermen's cove west of Aberdaron from which Colin Evans runs daily boat trips to the island.

We completed the two-mile crossing in fifteen minutes, powering over the water with gannets circling overhead. A porpoise appeared briefly, its dorsal fin cutting through the swell like a ploughshare, and then moments later we were out of the clutch of the roiling riptides and at rest in the harbour, a mere cleft in the rocks called Y Cafn (The Trough).

Waiting to greet us was an entire Hallelujah Chorus of seals. I counted at least 150 hauled out on the seaweed-smelling shores. Their mournful voices rose and fell on the wind, adding to the almost palpable sense of isolation.

There are no cars on Bardsey, no TV or mains electricity – only a handful of residents, a candy-striped lighthouse, a scattering of houses and farm buildings and a harbour-side boathouse. The springy turf, starred with wild flowers and untouched by commercial fertilisers, reminded me of the Outer Hebrides, and I could see why this has been a place of refuge since the dawn of Christianity.

For Evans, who has been bringing visitors here for eleven years, Bardsey has always had a special significance. This was where his grandfather lived and farmed, and where he spent every day of his school holidays. 'There's a soul and spirit here,' he said. 'It goes back ten thousand years and it has made me what I am.'

It was the Vikings who called it Bardsey – the Bards' Island; but its Welsh name is Ynys Enlli – 'the island of the tides' – a reference to the seven treacherous currents that separate it from the mainland. Reputed to be the burial place of twenty thousand saints, it was once a famous place of pilgrimage. Three journeys to Bardsey were considered equal to one visit to Rome. Now nothing remains except its medieval abbey ruins, and the island – four hundred acres of sheep-nibbled fields and a modest mountain called Mynydd Enlli – sleeps on, wrapped in dreams of the long ago, of Merlin entombed forever in a glass tower and nothing to disturb its ancient silence except the seals by day, and at night, wailing like souls from the

Celtic underworld, the eerie cries of Manx shearwaters returning to their burrows.

The shearwaters are ocean wanderers, spending the winter six thousand miles away off the coast of Brazil; but in springtime sixteen thousand pairs return to nest on Bardsey. By day the adults fly out to sea, boomeranging among the waves on outstretched wings, returning only at night to feed their chicks when the marauding gulls have gone to roost.

Bardsey is altogether a birdwatcher's heaven – hence the presence of the Bird and Field Observatory founded in 1953. Several pairs of choughs, the red-billed crows also known in Wales as *aderyn Arthur* – King Arthur's bird – breed every year. All kinds of rarities turn up on migration, including hoopoes and woodchat shrikes, and in recent years a forty-strong colony of puffins, perhaps an offshoot from the Gwylan Islands, have established themselves to the delight of visitors.

In summer the warm currents swirling around the Llyn Peninsula attract dense shoals of sand eels, the puffin's favourite prey, and with careful management there is no reason why these endearingly comical seabirds – also known as the clowns of the sea – should not continue to increase on Bardsey.

The island has been owned by the Bardsey Island Trust since 1979 and was declared a National Nature Reserve in 1986, but, as Evans was at pains to point out, there is more to Bardsey than wildlife conservation. 'You can still hear skylarks singing,' he said, 'but this is also a place where men still fish the seas and farm the land, maintaining a way of life that has lasted for centuries, and that is what makes it different from other Welsh islands. On Bardsey, people matter, too.'

Slow Train to Yesterday

St Ives, Cornwall, May 2011

B ack in the age of steam, before the railways were nationalised, the biggest moment of my year was the day we set off by train for our family holiday in Cornwall. Sometimes we travelled on the Atlantic Coast Express from Waterloo, speeding through the fields of Hampshire past trackside billboards bearing the slogan 'You are entering the Strong Country.'

How true, I thought in my innocence. That's where we are going: to King Arthur's land with its granite moors and rugged cliffs. Only when I was older did I realise the posters were advertising beer brewed by Strong's of Romsey.

But the greatest thrill of all was to board the Penzance-bound Cornish Riviera Express at Paddington, the London terminus of the Great Western Railway.

Whoever dreamed up the idea of the Cornish Riviera was a genius. Aided by evocative travel posters, it created an image of the Cornish coast as Britain's own Cote d'Azur, with its palm trees, artists and colourful fishing ports. Remember, this was long before the invention of package tours and cheap jet flights, in an age when the Mediterranean was still beyond reach of all but the wealthy. Yet, thanks to the Cornish Riviera Express, growing numbers of holiday visitors could be there in a matter of hours.

The Great Western Railway was established in the 1830s and its mainline route to Penzance pioneered by Isambard Kingdom Brunel, the top-hatted engineering prodigy of Victorian England.

It was above all a holiday line transporting summer visitors to the West Country, and the Cornish Riviera Express – known to all GWR staff as 'The Limited' – was its flagship service. In the glory days of steam its distinctive chocolate and cream carriages were hauled by King Class and Castle Class locomotives, seventy-nine-ton smoke-belching monsters built in Swindon and painted a glossy Brunswick Green. In those days it took six and a half hours to reach Penzance. But as I discovered on a voyage of childhood nostalgia, today's High Speed Trains (HSTs) have shortened the journey time to five hours.

On leaving Paddington, the first leg to Reading is almost dead level and the train rolls gently down the valley of the Kennet to Newbury and Hungerford. I gaze out of the window and the years fall away as I recall the excitement of spotting familiar landmarks such as the Westbury White Horse.

On we go, west with the light, chasing the sun past the Somerset Levels to Taunton, with the Quantock Hills rolling away to the north and the Wellington Monument beckoning from the Blackdowns on the other side of the track.

Next stop is Exeter St David's, the starting point for one of the most scenic mainline rail journeys in Britain. The best of it lies on the left-hand side, where the Turf Hotel signals the beginnings of the Exe estuary; but spare a glance to the right as you pass Powderham Castle's oaks and fallow deer.

Now the estuary opens out, revealing a mile-wide expanse of silver channels and shining mudflats alive with oystercatchers, and suddenly I am a child again, with my nose pressed to the corridor windows as we race along at the edge of the tideway.

As we skirt Cockwood's harbour the protective arm of Dawlish Warren appears, followed by the first longed-for sight of the English

Channel, its blue waters set off to perfection by the red cliffs of South Devon. To reach Teignmouth from here the line's Victorian builders had to burrow through endless layers of Permian sandstone – the leftover landscape of the age of dinosaurs – creating a succession of tunnels in which the train now plays hide and seek with the sea, and as we pass Hole Head I am relieved to see that the twin rock stacks known as the Parson and Clerk are still standing, although the outer rock, the Clerk, is much diminished, having been beheaded by a storm in 2003.

At Teignmouth we turn inland again, following the route of the migrating salmon as they head up the Teign estuary past Newton Abbot to their spawning redds in the Dartmoor combes. Here, in Devon's apple-blossom valleys, the primroses lie thick as clotted cream by every woodland edge.

The old-time express trains used to talk to the rails, beating out a clickety-clack rhythm as they huffed and puffed up Dainton Bank – the third steepest mainline incline in Britain. But today's streamlined HST diesels take it in their stride and we purr along as smooth as silk, crossing the River Dart at Totnes and hurrying on down to Plymouth with tantalising glimpses of Dartmoor to the north.

Now comes another special moment as Brunel's iconic Royal Albert Bridge carries us over the Tamar to Saltash. Painted grey as the warships in Devonport docks, this ironclad masterpiece opened in 1859, and when Brunel died that same year his name was placed on the portals at both ends of the bridge as a lasting memorial to the man who put the Great in Great Western.

To cross the Tamar is to travel out of England into another country, and to describe it as such is no longer hyperbole now that the Cornish people are to be officially recognised as a national minority on a par with the Scots, Welsh and Irish. On the other side of the river, as if to underline the point, Saltash station proudly greets passengers with a sign in Cornish. Kernow a'gas dynnergh, it says. Welcome to Cornwall.

On the eighty miles of track between Saltash and Penzance the old-time steam trains wound their way across more than forty viaducts – most of them conceived by Brunel to carry his precious line across Cornwall's wooded river valleys. Beyond Truro the woods give way to gorse-clad moors, and Carn Brea monument appears on its granite hilltop, brooding over a post-industrial landscape of abandoned tin mines. The hard-rock miners – the Cornish Jacks who followed the lodes deep underground – have long since departed, leaving their engine houses open to the sky; but the pride of the communities they left behind is still there, borne out by the sight of Baner Piran, the black and white Cornish flag of St Piran fluttering from a Redruth church tower.

At St Erth I chose to leave the Cornish Riviera Express to complete the last leg of its journey to Penzance, and await one last treat: the arrival of the two-coach shuttle service to St Ives.

The single-track branch line to St Ives was the last to be built to Brunel's 'broad gauge' specification. Opened in 1877, it was converted to standard gauge fifteen years later and was used mostly for transporting fish. Today its main cargo are holiday visitors, and although it takes only twelve minutes to complete the four and a half miles to St Ives, there is no lovelier rail journey in Britain; a slow train to yesterday, dawdling around the shell-sand beaches and dizzy clifftops of St Ives Bay.

As we come round the final curve, St Ives itself comes into view, a salt-encrusted barnacle of a town clinging to its knobbly promontory beside a picture-book harbour that has bewitched generations of painters. Bathed in dazzling Atlantic sea light, the whole town sparkles come rain or shine, and everything is as I remember it: herring gulls wailing over Porthminster sands, slate roofs smothered in yolk-yellow lichens, the smell of hot pasties in the granite lanes and Godrevy Lighthouse perched on the horizon, presiding over the bluest of bays.

First introduced in 1904, the Cornish Riviera Express rose to fame in the 1930s and still departs every morning from Paddington on its 305-mile journey to Penzance, the most westerly railway station in Britain.

In 2014, when the line was battered by a succession of ferocious winter storms, its very survival hung in the balance – just like the section of mainline track left dangling in mid-air when the sea wall at Dawlish was swept away in February. For eight long weeks the line was closed, isolating Cornwall and most of Devon while repairs took place, using six thousand tonnes of concrete and a hundred and fifty tonnes of steel to shore up the wall and repair the track at a cost of thirty-five million pounds. When the line was reopened miraculously ahead of schedule on 4 April, the collective sigh of relief could be heard right across the West Country.

Lullaby in Roseland

St Mawes, Cornwall, February 2010

In South Cornwall even in the dead of winter you can feel the mildness in the air. The first daffodils are out in December. Camellias bloom at Christmas and by February the subtropical gardens at Trebah and Glendurgan are already aglow with the miracle of the Cornish spring.

Tregony is where it all begins, on the upper reaches of the Fal. This is the gateway to Roseland, that beguiling peninsula of woods and creeks and National Trust beaches between St Mawes and Veryan Bay.

Crugsillick, Polhendra, Mellangoose, Ruan Lanihorne – let the poetry of its Celtic place names entice you along the back roads. In these lost lands between the woods and the water lies the true and mysterious heart of Cornwall, still dreaming of its Dark Age saints.

Out of season it is quiet as a prayer, its wooded valleys cobwebbed with lanes that burrow like badger runs between the trees, plunging down one-in-four gradients to emerge at last beside one of the tidal waterways whose salty fingers thrust far into the hinterland beneath the overhanging oaks.

These are the rias, the drowned river valleys that are South Cornwall's most characteristic feature. Formed when sea levels rose after the last Ice Age, they are a powerful reminder of what global warming could bring; and for me they always exude a special magic, especially in late autumn when the smell of fallen leaves combines with the tang of the tideways to bring on a nostalgia that cuts to the bone, recalling the Cornwall of my childhood.

Beside one such creek on the Fal estuary hides St Just-in-Roseland. Is there any village with a lovelier name? Or a more tranquil last resting place than its waterside churchyard, wrapped around with palms and camellias?

Sooner or later every road leads down to the coast, to the little fishing village of Portscatho whose cottages are as dazzling white as any Greek island village, or to Portloe, a cleft in the cliffs where the Lugger Hotel stands with its feet in the sea on a slipway covered in crab pots.

In the gaunt headlands of the Nare and the Dodman there is grandeur enough for all, but the south coast of Cornwall is gentler than the north. Its bays and coves are safe and sheltered and even the light is subtly different. On the north coast you stand with the sun at your back, but here at midday it shines in front of you, beating a path of hammered silver all the way to the horizon.

True, north Cornwall may have the surf but it's the south that has the style, and nowhere more so than at Rosevine, where the Driftwood Hotel – a vision of blue and cream Cape Cod clapboard – overlooks a quiet stretch of cormorant rocks and shining sand. The South West Coast Path runs past the bottom of the garden – a temptation too good to miss – and so I followed it down to Portscatho's pocket-sized harbour, tunnelling through jungles of wind-bent sloes. The strand line at Porthcurnick was strewn with limpets, but the sands themselves were deserted, although the Plume of Feathers, Portscatho's seventeenth-century pub, was full of ramblers.

At St Mawes, by far the best-known resort in Roseland, a high tide was slopping over the roadway. This is where visiting yachtsmen come to splash out at the Tresanton, Cornwall's swankiest seaside hotel; but those on a more modest budget might prefer to board the passenger ferry to Falmouth for a twenty-minute cruise across the finest sailing waters in the Southwest.

At the Prince of Wales Pier, I stepped ashore and made my way along Market Street towards the National Maritime Museum on Discovery Quay. There's a real buzz about the town nowadays, helped by the presence of ten thousand university students, and the museum itself is the perfect destination for a wet day. Among its exhibits is a pair of storm-damaged doors removed from the Bishop Rock lighthouse in 1994. Although they were built of solid bronze the waves crumpled them like paper, a chilling demonstration of the sea's unimaginable power.

After lunch it was back to the Pier for another ferry ride, this time up-river to Truro. The journey takes just over an hour and begins on the open waters of Carrick Roads, but once you have passed Restronguet Point the wind dies, the hills close in and the oaks steal down to the water's edge.

Upstream of the King Harry Ferry, mothballed container ships lie at their moorings, looking as out of place as blocks of flats among the pristine woodlands. On the west bank is Trelissick, one of the National Trust's flagship gardens; and on the other side stands the five-hundred-year-old Smugglers' Cottage at Tolverne where I had lunched earlier in the week.

The tea sold at Tolverne is grown on the nearby Tregothnan estate, the first place in Britain with its own plantation. The first bushes were planted in 1999 and thrive in a climate akin to Darjeeling's. But the creeper-clad cottage has another claim to fame, for it was here during World War II that General Eisenhower addressed 27,000

American troops before they embarked for the D-Day landings. His chair is preserved in an upstairs room.

Cruising up the Fal's sheltered waters it would be easy to imagine that the whole of South Cornwall is as gentle as this, but a trip to the Lizard will soon change your mind. Here on the southernmost point of mainland Britain stands the Lizard Light, warning shipping to steer clear of a savage coast whose names alone – Vellan Drang, Ogo Dour, the Manacles – are enough to strike dread into the heart of any fogbound mariner. Deep South this may be, but when the winter storms come beating in it is as wild as anything the Atlantic coast can throw at you.

I went there on a glorious day, but even then at Kynance Cove a big sea was running, the swell exploding in huge shell bursts against the serpentine rocks of Asparagus Island. Out of the wind with my back against a rock I sat and picnicked while gulls wailed in the abyss below and a pair of choughs – breeding again after an absence of fifty years – whirled and tumbled in the up-draughts. Quintessential Cornwall at its best.

Lord of the Flies

Lifton, Devon, September 1977

A fine rain falls on the West Country. Long convoys of washed-out campers are beating a hasty retreat up the A30. Dartmoor is disappearing into the drizzle and Roy Buckingham is cursing the weather again. 'What we need,' he says, 'is a really nice cloudburst.'

In spite of the summer that never was, West Country rivers have been running low and fishermen have been praying for salmon weather. They want the Tamar in full spate for the big fish to run in from the sea on their life's last journey to the spawning grounds. When the water has calmed and cleared, every holding pool between Gunnislake and Launceston has its fish. Not stale salmon, whose rusty flanks show they have lain too long in the river, but fresh-run fish, silver bright with the bloom of the sea still on them.

Roy Buckingham is a wiry Cornishman who caught his first salmon when he was thirteen, went on to become a champion fly-caster and now works as chief instructor and head bailiff for the Arundell Arms at Lifton, a creeper-clad fishing inn with twenty miles of the finest sporting waters in the Southwest. In the past eight years he has taught two thousand people to fish, but today he has really set himself a task: to help me catch my first salmon.

Legs entombed in waders, we swish through mushroom-smelling meadows to the junction pool where two rivers, Lyd and Tamar, meet in the shade of a patriarch oak. Luckily there is no one to watch my first shot at fly-casting. 'It's easy,' says Buckingham encouragingly.

'Just like knocking a nail in a wall.' But the fly is wicked sharp and the silky hiss as it flicks past my ear is more than a shade disconcerting.

The idea, Buckingham explains, is to fish the pool from neck to tail, first with a fly and then with a spinner, covering all the spots where a fish might lie. From a casket of lures he chooses an artificial fly called Thunder and Lightning. It rests lightly in his palm, a thing of bristling deadly beauty. Stiff orange hackles sprout from its throat. Tinsel and black ostrich herl adorn its silk body. Its wings are a bouquet of feathers: golden pheasant, guinea fowl, jungle cock and mallard – all this to tempt the most fastidious of appetites.

For this is the most astounding fact about the salmon: it never feeds once it enters the river. Why, then, will a fasting salmon take a fly? It could be a simple reflex action, the leftover response of a sea-going predator that has spent months scoffing krill on the Greenland Banks. Or it could be no more than an act of annoyance. Either way, our luck hangs on the choice of just the right lure.

Midday now, and the oakwood valley is as quiet as a church. A dipper darts downstream. The rain has stopped and dragonflies are skimming over the stickle of fast water in the throat of the pool. But no fish come.

No luck with the fly, so we set aside the twelve-foot split-cane rod for a smaller spinning rod. Hours melt like minutes, lost in a reverie of river lore, in the repetitive flick of the rod's end and the steady winding-in of the spinner.

When it happens it comes as a shock. It feels as if the hook has stuck fast in a rock – until the rock takes off downstream and Buckingham is yelling at me to keep the rod up. The visceral thrill of that first thumping rush is indescribable; it's like trying to rein in a runaway horse.

Now from deep down comes a sudden blossoming of light, a golden scythe blade swinging through the pool's dark mystery. I pump him closer. There is a thrashing and a shaking, and then the net is under him. The last rites with a cosh, called a priest, and it's all over.

It is a six-pound grilse – a youngster returned to the Tamar after one winter at sea – with the characteristic hook-jawed profile of a cock fish. The credit for catching him must go to Roy Buckingham. Beginner's luck? Put it down to whichever river god you believe in. But I have the memory – and a fish in the freezer.

Dartmoor's Dark Age Undercroft

Wistman's Wood, Devon, December 1984

Dartmoor has always been a place apart. Raised above the rest of Devon, it is the last great wilderness in southern Britain, aloof and withdrawn – high country where the sky feels closer and it is possible to walk for miles over bare brown hills and seldom meet a soul. Dartmoor is haunted, bittersweet and poignant; one minute an aching emptiness of peat hag and heather, the next a deep valley at your feet, a falling away of mossy oaks, the sudden gleam of a salmon river. But above all it is granite country, stern and rain-swept; a world of cleaves, clitters, tors and quakers – Dartmoor vernacular for glens, screes, inselbergs and oozing bogs. Its hillsides are littered with relics of forgotten people. Bronze Age circles and grizzled monoliths stand marooned in seas of dying bracken.

Older still is Wistman's Wood. On the Ordnance Survey map it is simply a small green teardrop in the valley of the West Dart above Two Bridges; but trees of any kind are rare on Dartmoor, and a broad-leaved wood at 1,400 feet is almost a miracle.

The day had started bright and benign. At Drewsteignton it had been almost warm enough to sit outside in the village square, but it did not last. On the high moor the sun vanished and a cold wind blew. Cloud thickened from the west and all colour drained from the landscape.

In the valley below, riders were moving in single file. Their scarlet coats shone like sparks against the dun sloes, and the sound of a hunting horn drifted up on the wind, thin and insistent, calling to hounds as they sought a fox in the furze under Merripit Hill.

The path from Two Bridges was easy to follow. Blobs of yellow paint splashed on rocks marked the way across the fields. At the head of the valley Crow Tor glowered on the skyline, guarding the West Dart's boggy birthplace, and a mile and a half after leaving the road I entered the wood.

The most remarkable feature of Wistman's Wood is its lack of height. It is composed almost entirely of ancient pedunculate oaks, each one so gnarled and stunted that few exceed fifteen feet. It is a troll wood, sinister and storm-stricken, a pagan grove whose close-knit canopy conceals a tumbling chaos of mossy boulders and slabs of moorstone as big as grand pianos. Woodrush and polypody ferns thrive everywhere in its damp gloom; and every tree, each dwarfish trunk and wizened limb, is lagged with lichen. In woodland terms it is a living monument as precious as any parish church; and if Chiltern beechwoods can be likened to Gothic cathedrals, then Wistman's Wood is a Dark Age undercroft.

By any reckoning it is one of the seven wonders of the moor, and many writers have been drawn to it. The earliest description is by Tristram Risdon. Writing in 1620, he named it as one of Dartmoor's three most memorable sights, but its pedigree is much older. Crossing's 1912 *Guide to Dartmoor* suggests two possible earlier versions of its name, both of which would suggest a history of at least a thousand years. One, *Uisg maen coed*, is Celtic and means the Stony Wood by the Water. The other, Wealasman's Wood, is Saxon, but means the Wood of the Celts; and in living memory there were still moor-folk who called it Welshman's Wood.

Until the twentieth century the wood was so dense and low growing that it was almost impenetrable, inhabited only by foxes that made their lairs beneath its rocks. There hounds could not follow nor huntsmen dislodge them, even with crowbars and terriers.

Since then, grazing and greater public access to the moor have opened it up to such an extent that the Nature Conservancy Council, which manages the wood as a nature reserve, is concerned for its future. Like so many natural features of the countryside it is unwittingly being damaged by innocent visitors, and in time unrestricted access may no longer be possible. Already the NCC has fenced off an experimental plot to monitor the changes that occur when grazing animals and trampling humans are excluded.

Inside the wood, no birds sang. The acid colours of the mosses shone out in sharp counterpoint to the dead bracken. The trees had long since pensioned off their leaves, which lay now, piled up in the hollows between the rocks. Rotted by winter rain, they would provide rich humus for next year's flowers: wood sorrel, foxglove, herb Robert and tormentil.

I did not go deep into the wood. The words of the NCC rang in my ears: 'The vegetation is fragile and deteriorating; please help us to protect it.' Instead I sat on a mossy moorstone slab beneath the twisted trees, listened to the infant River Dart hissing down the valley, and thought it one of the most hallowed places in Britain.

Cul-de-Sac Country

Hartland, Devon, August 1997

Hartland is the West Country's Empty Quarter, a lonely triangle of tranquillity between Bude and Bideford. The thin end of the wedge is Hartland Point, driven into seas of unimaginable ferocity. It belongs in North Devon but still has a Cornish feel about it; cul-de-sac country, threaded by lanes that lead to nowhere, ending abruptly above the Atlantic.

In the days of sail, few stretches of coast were held in such dread as Hartland's forsaken cliffs, where huge waves come beating in all the way from Newfoundland. 'From Padstow Point to Lundy Light is a sailor's grave by day and night,' ran the old West Country rhyme, and it's true. Stand here in the teeth of a westerly gale when a heavy sea is running and the rollers explode against the cliffs with a sound like heavy artillery, and Hartland can seem like the wildest place on earth. Yet out of the wind, in the short, steep-sided, oakwood valleys that run westward to the sea, the climate is as soft as Madeira, with cuckoo flowers blooming in damp streamside meadows, encouraging the creation of dreamy gardens such as the one at Docton Mill.

Villages are few and seem happy to keep a low profile among the high fields of the hinterland. Ask the millions of visitors who descend every summer on the West Country: who has ever heard of Bradworthy? Or Woolfardisworthy (pronounced 'Woolsery' by the locals)? Blank looks are the usual response. Even Kilkhampton, on the road between Bude and Clovelly, seldom registers, despite a church filled with monuments to the Grenvilles, local heroes whose numbers included Sir Richard Grenville of the *Revenge*.

To reach North Devon's Great Unknown I drove north from Bude's surf beaches and pasty shops, through Poughill, where I was evacuated during World War II, passing the fifteenth-century church where I was taken every Sunday by horse and cart. The farm where I spent two years of my wartime childhood has since been converted to holiday cottages, but the lanes were still as I remembered, their blackthorn bushes backcombed into witches' locks by the streaming winter gales.

A signpost bearing the name of Duckpool seemed too good to miss. It steered me down a valley thick with oaks. There were primroses and orange-tip butterflies in the lanes and the air was heavy with the garlic breath of ramson flowers. Beyond the oaks rose sweeps of gorse, framing a bay of black rocks.

I picnicked in Coombe Valley woods, with ravens grunting overhead; then drove on to Morwenstow, Cornwall's northernmost parish: a scatter of isolated farms and a church dedicated to Morwenna, a Saxon saint. In the nineteenth century, Morwenstow's vicar was the eccentric R. S. Hawker, who wore sea boots to church and once sat on a rock in Bude dressed as a mermaid, with his head covered in seaweed. The hut where he spent hours staring out to sea, writing poetry and smoking opium, still stands on Vicarage Cliff. Built from the washed-up timbers of drowned ships, it now belongs to the National Trust and must be the smallest property in its portfolio of historic buildings.

In Parson Hawker's secluded churchyard stands the ghostly white figure of a kilted clansman, claymore in hand, arising from a sea of celandines. It is the figurehead from the *Caledonia*, a two-hundred-ton brig from Arbroath, wrecked on the rocks in 1843, and marks the grave of her captain and crew. Hawker was forever scouring the coast for sailors' corpses. Many were headless, decapitated on Hartland's cruel reefs, but all received a Christian burial.

At Marsland Mouth, a mile or so north of Morwenstow, the little Marsland stream emerges from a deep valley between sloping waves of gorse, defining an ancient frontier that once divided Celt from Saxon. Where the stream ran out across the pebbles, I stood astride it on the beach, one foot in Cornwall and the other in Devon. To the north, the long-distance coastal footpath toiled up the cliff towards Knap Head and Embury Beacon. Inland, to the east of the A30, Hartland's only main road, two of the West Country's greatest rivers have their beginnings. One is the Torridge, Tarka the Otter's home waters, flowing into Bideford Bay. The other is the Tamar, which marks the border between Devon and Cornwall as it runs down to Plymouth Sound. Between the hamlets of East and West Youlstone it trickles through a kingcup marsh, scarcely deep enough to hide a brook trout. Yet in its lower reaches it is big enough to float a battleship.

In Hartland village, three miles from Clovelly, there was scarcely a visitor to be seen. It reminded me of Ireland: a 1950s time warp of peeling, whitewashed cottages, pubs and grocers' shops, with a dog asleep in the middle of the road.

Lower down the valley stands Stoke church, with its tall stone tower, numbered pews for six hundred worshippers and wonderful four-hundred-year-old carved oak rood screen. History oozes from its every pore. The church is dedicated to St Nectan, a fifth-century Welsh hermit, and was founded by Countess Gytha, the mother of King Harold, in thanksgiving for the life of her husband, Earl Godwin, who survived a shipwreck on the Hartland coast.

To see how lucky he was you have only to visit Hartland Quay, looking out across a desolation of savage reefs and shark-fin rocks. It says much about the power of the sea that the original quay was swept away during a storm in 1896.

A solitary, salt-stained hotel displayed handwritten notices imploring visitors to wipe the tar from their shoes before entering the Wreckers Retreat bar; but I chose to picnic on the surrounding clifftops, listening to the frantic piping calls of oystercatchers in the cove below, and a peregrine screaming over an abyss of shadow.

All down this western side of Hartland the coast is being tested to destruction. Much of it is inherently unstable, constantly crumbling and breaking away, exposing the tortured strata to provide an object lesson in geology. Follow the coast path south and you pass giant slabs keeled over at forty-five degrees. Ahead looms St Catherine's Tor, a turf-clad pyramid with its face torn away on the seaward side. Elsewhere you can see where the buckled strata have collapsed like a deck of cards, or where their upended edges run out into the sea like black knife-blades, ripping the incoming waves to shreds.

At Speke's Mill Mouth, geology students were scribbling notes beside a stream that plunged in a single white plume for eighty feet on to the beach below. Beyond, the path snaked steeply up a green crest to Longpeak, then away past Sandhole Cliff and Gull Rock, every step more dramatic than the last.

Yet even here, Hartland has its softer moods. To reach Hartland Point itself I drove down a lane with grass growing in the middle of it. Haze blurred the horizon, so that I could not make out where the sea ended and the sky began.

It was April, the time of the blackthorn winter, and the clifftops were frosted white with blossom. Larks were singing over the bare fields, and as I followed the coast path to Damehole Point the air was filled with migrating swallows that dived around me in a constant, joyous stream as if to celebrate their safe return.

All I Ask Is a Tall Ship

Fowey, Cornwall, August 1980

We set sail after dark on St Swithin's Day, but there was no rain; only shoals of stars, enmeshed in thickets of spars and rigging as we stole out of Fowey Harbour on the evening tide. Closing time in the King of Prussia; a rousing chorus of beery farewells from the quayside, and the bellowed response from Plum at the wheel. 'Goodbye my handsomes' echoing across the water. The voyage of the *Beagle* had begun.

Beagle she may be to everyone who saw the BBC's epic series 'The Voyage of Charles Darwin', but her real name is the *Marques*. Built in Spain in 1915, she began life as a sturdy pitch-pine workhorse tramping the Mediterranean with cargoes of fruit and almonds. Then, in 1972, an Englishman, Robin Cecil-Wright, bought her and brought her to Cornwall where, after starring in the *Onedin Line* series, she was converted from a two-masted brigantine to a three-masted barque to play the part of HMS *Beagle*, complete with poop deck, gun ports and beagle figurehead.

Now the *Marques* was setting out once more from her home port of Fowey, this time on an eighty-three-day round-Britain voyage organised by a human dynamo called Richard Demarco, director of the Demarco art gallery in Edinburgh. Edinburgh Arts 1980, as Demarco calls this current circumnavigation of Britain, is a kind of ocean-going prelude to the Edinburgh Festival, and the voyage has been planned so that the *Marques* will arrive in the Firth of Forth during the Festival later this month.

My fellow shipmates were a mixed bag: art students and army officers, painters, professors, wives and girlfriends. Like me they had signed on for the first leg of the voyage, from Fowey to Bristol via Penzance.

There was also a captain, Mark Lichfield, casually elegant, ex-Royal Navy, co-owner of the *Marques*, and a professional crew. To call them motley would fail to do them justice. Barefoot in all weathers and dressed for the most part in disintegrating denims, they swung through the rigging like demented gibbons. Daggers and marlinspikes dangled from their waists. They bristled with beards and Cornish accents. In short, they looked a villainous bunch – and were the kindest, the most patient, the most humorous and hard-working crew you could wish to meet.

Richard Demarco believes with messianic fervour in the concept of the artist as explorer, and the itinerary is laced with a strong measure of art galleries, abbeys and standing stones. Ashore at Penzance, we made a pilgrimage to the Penwith Gallery in St Ives and drove over the moors in an open-topped bus to meet the painter Patrick Heron.

But the main attraction for everyone aboard was the *Marques* herself; and for ordinary people she was the last chance to experience life aboard a romantic square-rigger from the age of sail.

The price you pay for this unique privilege is not cheap. A passage on the *Marques* means dirty hands and wet feet, damp bunks in cabins more like broom cupboards and, for poor sailors, the urgent delivery of your last meal over the leeward side. (A shame, because meals on board the *Marques* are huge and wholesome.)

Divided into four watches (named Darwin, Fitzroy, Wickham and Sullivan after members of the original *Beagle* crew), volunteers help the crew to sail the ship, taking turns at the wheel, going aloft and wrestling with the complexities of sheets, buntings, clews and halyards. The work is hard but the rewards are immeasurable: companionship and a gratifying sense of wellbeing that only effort and endurance can forge.

Kennelled in Penzance harbour by overnight gales, we sailed next morning in heavy seas, plunging eagerly into Mount's Bay before bearing away to the west. Beyond Tater Du lighthouse we set jibs and spanker, rounding the Runnel Stone Reef, where a lurching buoy moaned in the drizzle like a lost bullock. Then we changed course again, and with the wind behind us I joined the topmen and went aloft to unfurl the square sails: main and fore course, topsails and t'gallant sails.

In this manner, flying every inch of canvas, we charged on at even greater speed, the *Marques* rising and falling among the grey hills and hollows of the sea, her salt-stained sails hauled taut in a wild pattern of sweeping parabolas, swinging and filling against the wild sky.

Away to starboard lay Land's End, the thin end of the wedge that is Cornwall, driven home between the English Channel and the Atlantic Ocean. A terrifying seascape of haggard headlands, of cliffs torn asunder and wave-smashed rocks with grim-sounding names: Folly Cove, the Armed Knight, Zawn Kellys. Land's End itself may be tawdry and turf-worn to those who visit it, but seen from the heaving deck of a square-rigged sailing vessel it seems like the most savage place on earth: the English Cape Horn.

'Delight,' wrote Charles Darwin, 'is a weak term to express the feelings of a naturalist who, for the first time, has wandered by himself in a Brazilian forest.' It is also inadequate when trying to express my own feelings as someone who, for the first time, had manned the yards aboard the *Marques*. No wonder she stopped the traffic as we sailed up the Clifton Gorge to Bristol at the end of the voyage.

EAST

And nigh this toppling reed, still as the dead
The great pike lies, the murderous patriarch
Watching the waterpit shelving the dark,
Where through the plash his lithe bright vassals thread.

from The Pike *by Edmund Blunden*

The Old Man of Brundon

Stour Valley, Suffolk, January 1984

Suffolk lay silent under a leaden sky. Last night six inches of snow smothered the Stour Valley. Later it rained, reducing the pristine fields to crust, though a dull carapace of ice still covered Borley Mill pool. But now, as I followed the river downstream to Brundon, the air held a hint of more snow to come.

The Stour Valley is low and undulating country where distance is measured in hundred-acre fields and horizons marked by lonely church towers. Between Long Melford and Sudbury it becomes Gainsborough's England, home of the painter, who was born in Sudbury in 1727. But today, under snow, its wintry landscapes were as bleak as Breughel.

The Stour rises at the border of Suffolk and Cambridgeshire on Wratting Common, where the London clay runs up against the spring line of the East Anglian chalk; and for most of the eighty-odd miles down to its estuary beyond Manningtree it is willow country. Commonest is the crack willow, *Salix fragilis*, whose twigs come away with a snap when pulled; but the wet alluvial soils are also ideal for the majestic white willow, *Salix alba*, which can drink four hundred gallons a day when fully grown, and its close relative the bat willow, *S. alba caerulea*, whose solid, silky wood is carved into cricket bats.

Summer and winter, the Stour is a cold river; its temperature seldom varies more than a few degrees. Recent floods had left sodden tidemarks of straw and dead wood along the banks and the river was still high. Under the trees it was a dark bottle green, swollen with meltwater from the streaming ditches. It is a good river to fish, clean and slow, with deep pools and long swims between rippling tresses of submerged weed.

Somewhere down there furtive chub would be moving, heavy and blunt-mouthed among the drowning tree roots, with fat carp and tench rooting for bloodworms in the muddy bottom like pigs after acorns; and maybe, lurking among the reeds, the shadow of a hungry pike.

Best for pike are the spots where the old millraces have scoured pools up to thirty feet deep in places; and in one such hole lives the legendary pike known as the Old Man of Brundon. The miller who lived at Borley Mill until 1970 would often talk of the 'gurt luce' (Suffolk dialect for a great pike) that patrolled the river between here and Brundon. Pike have a fondness for cruising just below the surface; and sometimes the miller, half glimpsing a sudden movement in the water, would turn in time to see a huge, recumbent shape, like a dappled log, sinking back into the darkness.

In 1971 the mill changed hands. It was bought by Rupert Brown, a book designer, who dismissed rumours of a giant pike as local folklore. But the following year he found a dead swan floating in the mill pool. It was headless and had an enormous bite on its thigh. 'No otter could have left such marks,' said Brown. 'They could have been made only by the jaws of a big fish with eye teeth as long as an Alsatian's.' Since then he has seen the monster on several occasions; and once he met a white-faced angler, his tackle smashed, who thought he must have hooked a seal.

So the legend of the Old Man of Brundon has continued to grow, while the fish itself, heavier and more cunning with each passing year, is now thought to weigh close on forty pounds. It can be recognised by a split pectoral fin on its left side. 'That had to be the Old Man,' the miller would exclaim. 'I see'd the cleft fin.' But no fisherman had ever succeeded in landing him. Now he was a veteran, maybe half a century old, which meant that he had probably been patrolling this same stretch of river since before I was born. It was a strange thought.

I had first heard about the Old Man of Brundon the previous summer when I had come down to Borley to write an article for the *Sunday Times Magazine* about a new book that Rupert Brown was designing with Martin Knowelden, the wildlife artist.

As a fish painter, Knowelden is supreme. With pencil and paintbrush he can capture a fish better than anyone, and preserve it in oils with every reed and ripple of its mysterious world intact. He had seen the Old Man that spring. 'He was huge,' he said. 'Come back in the winter and we'll try and catch him.'

I had no illusions that we would succeed. Nor did I particularly wish to see the legend reduced to a varnished carcass, stuffed with sawdust and staring glassy-eyed from a trophy case. But regardless of the swollen river and the snow that had begun to fall afresh, Martin was determined that we should fish for pike. So, legs entombed in Wellingtons and waterproofs, we trudged along the bank until we found a pool where a small brook joined the river. There, Martin knew, the water was a good seven feet deep and the far bank bristled with bulrushes, whose submerged stems offer perfect cover for pike.

We carried two rods. One was eleven feet long, a slender thing of hollow glass. That would be used to ledger or dead-bait for the Old Man, using snap tackle on a wire trace, with two treble hooks and a sprat from the freezer. The other was a nine-foot glass spinning-rod with a plug painted to resemble a small pickerel. If the plug was jerked through the murky water, a pike might sense the uneven vibrations and mistake the movements for those of a sick or wounded fish.

Martin took the big rod first and cast the dead-bait downstream with a finely judged flick that dropped it in about five feet of water, so that the sprat would lie on the bottom below a small red pike bob. Then he slackened the ratchet on the reel and set the rod to rest.

Now began the long wait. The river flowed past in slow, viscous coils and I watched the red bob as if mesmerised, willing it to dip under the weight of a fish; but it never moved.

Meanwhile, the life of the river returned to normal. A moorhen emerged from a ditch and padded across the white fields on outsize feet. A dabchick came drifting past with the current before diving and reappearing lower downstream. A kingfisher settled briefly on a low branch, glittering like an electric spark and then whirring downriver with a shrill whistle. 'Angling is such a marvellous way of observing wildlife,' said Martin. 'On a walk, all you see is a circle of fearful or fleeing birds and animals. But once you sit still, life goes on again as if you weren't there.'

We sat hunched like herons, but the cold bit to the marrow and we were forced to stand up and move around to keep warm. No luck with the dead-bait, so Martin took up the smaller spinning rod. An hour passed, lost in total concentration, in the repetitive flick of the rod's end, the mechanical winding in of the plug.

By now the snow was falling steadily in fat, wet flakes, shutting out the distant hedgerows. My thoughts began to wander. I thought of the first time I had come to Borley. It had been early summer, with the smell of may blossom pouring across the meadows in sultry tides, and I had sat on the bank and watched the tarnished gleam of shoaling chub as they cruised in the sun-warmed shallows below the mill.

I thought of the carp I had eaten last winter in Yugoslavia, skewered on a willow stick, basted with olive oil and cooked over the embers of a wood fire in the marshes of Hutovo Blato; and the giant carp in our own British waters, and the stoical fanatics who fish for them by night, alone in the all-embracing silence of the dark. I thought of the pike with its shovel snout and wolfish teeth, every inch a predator.

And still no warning movement from the small red bob. I tried to guess what was happening in that secret world beneath the surface as the rich taint of sprat drifted down with the current. Somewhere, surely, a pike must be lurking, cold eyes unblinking. Perhaps the Old Man himself, heavy with the weight of years, watching, waiting…

When it happened it was a total surprise; my daydreams were shattered by the reel's urgent scream. Already Martin had dived for the rod and was stripping off more line as the tip jumped and the bob went under. When the line slackened briefly, he tightened the ratchet and struck once, against the pull, setting the barbs in the gristle of the fish's jaw. At once the rod curved taut as the pike took off in a violent dash to try to rid itself of the tormenting hook.

Three minutes passed. The fish was tiring. As it lost the power of its caudal muscles it began to roll in the water, and for the first time we could see it, a greenish blossoming of light, a heavy body swinging like a scythe blade, and a broad, flapping tail. It wasn't the Old Man of Brundon but it was a good fish all the same. There was a thrashing and a shaking, and then Martin had the keep net under, and up she came, a fresh, deep-bellied hen. An eleven-pounder, we discovered later, and in Martin's words, 'a welcome addition to the deep freeze'. Carefully he removed the hooks with surgical forceps. A swift *coup de grâce* with the priest (a fisherman's cosh) – and it was all over.

Arthur Ransome's Secret Tideways

Walton Backwaters, Essex, June 2010

In the seaside town of Walton-on-the-Naze I drove along the promenade, turned off down a cindery track where tattooed men in oily jeans preside over a graveyard of junked cars, and came face to face with an Essex I thought had gone for ever.

The Walton Backwaters lie beyond Colchester at the outermost end of the county, between the Colne and Stour estuaries, where the rolling cornfields of the Tendring Peninsula slide into the North Sea. This was the setting for *Secret Water*, the 1930s children's classic written by Arthur Ransome of *Swallows and Amazons* fame. Little has changed since Ransome himself sailed here in the *Nancy Blackett*, his twenty-eight-foot gaff-rigged cutter, and today its seven thousand acres of mudflats, saltmarsh and glittering creeks are preserved as the Hamford Water National Nature Reserve, managed by Natural England and the Essex Wildlife Trust.

It's a tide-ruled world, half marsh, half sky, with nothing but a pencil-thin horizon to determine where they meet; and unless you own a boat yourself there is only one way to get to grips with it.

Step forward Tony Haggis, an Essex boatman born and bred, who is waiting for me with *Karina* down at Walton's Foundry Jetty.

Karina is an Essex girl with a difference. Broad in the beam, she is Tony's pride and joy, a buxom twenty-one-foot ex-Trinity House ship's lifeboat converted for two-hour wildlife cruises. Haggis himself is in his late fifties, and don't be fooled by his Nepalese hat (acquired on his winter travels). He is an unreconstructed East Saxon with a beard like hoar frost and a wicked twinkle in his eye. Give him a battle-axe and he could pass for a Viking from central casting. For thirty-two years (apart from a couple of spells as a Greenpeace volunteer) he fished for sea bass and North Sea cod, a profession still followed by three of his four brothers, like their father before them. 'The last family in Walton still fishing,' he says proudly. But a back injury forced him to seek a gentler living, operating wildlife boat trips instead.

We set off north along Walton Channel, past Hedge End Island and a muddy creek called the Dardanelles, past mooring buoys and lines of yachts with names like *Strewth* and *Yellow Welly*. In the distance I can just make out the dockside cranes of Felixstowe, leaning against the skyline like a herd of giraffes that have just spotted a lion.

The saltings are still brown after the harshest winter in decades, but come summer they will once again be smothered in a mauve haze of sea lavender. The day is bright – this is the driest part of England – and the huge marshland skies are alive with birds, with the scream of gulls, the sad cries of redshanks. Black and white avocets sit tight on their eggs. A breeding colony of little terns erupts in a sudden flurry of snowflakes, and beyond Cormorant Creek as we round the corner of Horsey Island (Ransome called it Swallow Island), Haggis points out a marsh harrier sailing towards us on outspread pinions.

Across the broad reaches of Hamford Water we spot two round, sleek heads bobbing among the wavelets. Two pairs of liquid brown eyes return our gaze, soft and trusting as a Labrador's. 'Anyone seen seals before?' asks Haggis. Somebody nods. They have watched them on the Norfolk coast. 'Ah, but these are different. These are Essex seals,' quips Haggis. 'The females are all pregnant.'

But he is good on his facts, too. Tells us there are two species here, the common and Atlantic grey seal, co-existing in perfect harmony. Points out how the common seals' fur has been dyed a rich foxy red due to iron oxide in the mud, and explains how their pups can swim almost from birth.

On our way back past Bramble Island we cross the Wade, a stretch of open water between Horsey and the mainland. Haggis prods a boathook over the side to show how shallow it is – no more than three feet under our bows. At low water the Wade dries out completely, allowing Horsey's owners a brief window in which to drive across before the tide returns.

Back on shore again I made for the Naze Tower, an octagonal brick lighthouse put up in 1720 by Trinity House to warn sailors away from the treacherous offshore shoals. The crumbling cliffs on which it stands are stuffed with sharks' teeth and other fossils laid down fifty-five million years ago, but are being gobbled up by the sea at the rate of six feet a year. When the tower was built it stood a quarter of a mile inland. Now it is only fifty yards from the cliff edge and would have fallen into the sea within the next twenty-five years had its future not been secured by the £1.2 million Naze Heritage Project. In the 1970s it stood derelict until Roy Bradley, a musician with the Nitwits Band, bought it as a present for his wife. He planned to hoist a grand piano to the roof, but when that proved to be impossible the tower changed hands again and opened to the public for the first time in 2004.

The view from the top is worth the climb – a gull's-eye panorama that puts the entire mosaic of the Walton marshes into perspective more effectively than any map.

Afterwards, to round off the day, I drove up to Harwich for a whistle-stop tour around what David Whittle, vice-chairman of the Harwich Society, calls 'one of the best-kept secrets in Essex'.

He's right, too. I had imagined Harwich to be a vast seaport heaving with container ships and continental ferries. Instead, hidden behind the waterfront I found a quiet little town oozing with salty maritime history. Its three main streets run north to south, following the grid plan set down in medieval times, and across them run narrow, dogleg alleys designed to keep out the notorious East Anglian wind.

Here lived Christopher Jones, master of the *Mayflower*. His house still stands in King's Quay Street. Nelson enjoyed a tryst with Emma at the Three Cups Inn and Samuel Pepys was the local MP when Harwich was the HQ for the King's Navy.

What a sight it must have been a century ago when Harwich Quay was lined with bawleys – East Coast sailing craft designed for catching shrimps and whitebait. Or earlier still when the old Naval Dockyard was building men o' war, including the seventy-four-gun *Conqueror* that fought at Trafalgar.

One of the most distinctive buildings is the blue-and-white-painted Pier Hotel, overlooking the Ha'Penny Pier, a wooden Victorian structure named after the price of admission when it was built in 1837. Owned by Paul Milsom of Le Tolbooth fame, this is the place to push the boat out. Splash out if you can on the Mayflower Suite with its brass telescope and wide picture windows overlooking the waters where the Orwell flowing down from Ipswich meets the Stour on its way from Constable's England. From here you can watch the continental ferries sliding past like ocean-going tower blocks on their way upriver to Parkeston Quay, with Suffolk lying on the opposite shore like another country.

Then take yourself off to the Harbourside, the Pier Hotel's upstairs restaurant with its polished pewter bar, and treat yourself to champagne and oysters (local, of course), followed by lobster or sea bass expertly prepared by head chef Chris Oakley, who has been here since it opened in 1978. Essex doesn't get much better than this.

Holding Back the Deluge

Ely, Cambridgeshire, January 1990

The Fens of East Anglia, deep-drained and embanked against the sea, are one of the most mysterious places in Britain. Their open skies and wide horizons exert a powerful magic and reflect an epic chapter in the making of the English landscape. They contain some of the richest agricultural land anywhere in Europe and yet they are haunted by the fear of their oldest enemy – the rising sea.

Never was this fear more apparent in recent times than on 25 January 1990, when the great hurricane that came to be known as the Burns' Day Storm swept across southern Britain, felling thousands of trees and killing scores of people before rampaging on across the North Sea. The level fields of Cambridgeshire were freshly stitched with winter wheat. Brimming dykes ran out to the horizon. Ely Cathedral, the giant stone ship of the Fens, lay at anchor on its low ridge above the richest, flattest land in England, and by chance I was there when it happened.

From Quanea Drove, just outside Ely, I watched the storm blow in from the west. For one brief moment the sun broke through the scudding cloud. Its bleak light washed over the cathedral's Gothic tower, picking out Alan of Walsingham's glorious medieval Octagon against a sky as black as Fenland peat.

All day the wind howled across East Anglia, smashing fences, ripping off roofs; but Ely Cathedral stood firm, as it had done so many times before in its thousand years of history.

But this storm was different. It was the forerunner of a series of freak hurricanes that strayed from their normal path and tracked south, causing untold havoc in Britain and other parts of Europe.

Scientists believe these rogue winds are the result of global warming and predict a greater incidence of the killer storms endured by Britain in recent years. If they are right, the implications for low-lying areas such as the Cambridgeshire Fens are serious indeed. Some time within the next fifty years, as the greenhouse effect begins to bite, a combination of rising sea levels and a major storm surge could overwhelm Britain's coastal defences and rewrite the map of East Anglia overnight.

In the Fens the theory that the Earth is flat is entirely believable. No hills or crags disturb the illimitable distance. Here geological time is measured by the slow drip of sediment, the laying down of peat and the rise and fall of mighty floods. In the Fens the flatness of the land is its own monument to an endless struggle against the deluge, played out against huge horizons that seldom lie more than a few feet above the waiting sea.

The people who live and work here are a breed apart: stoic, independent, inward-looking. 'You have to remember this has always been a very isolated part of England,' said Mike Hollingsworth of the Ely National Farmers' Union. 'For centuries Ely was an island of monks and reed-cutters, and even today the feeling of being out on a limb persists.'

Graham Swift, the author of *Waterland*, is not a Fenman, yet his novel perfectly captures the elusive spirit of the place. 'North of Ely, south of King's Lynn; that was my Waterland,' he says. 'It was a fictional setting but one that related to the physical geography of the Fens. It's not a country I love, but it is very haunting. It exerts a strange compulsion. It gets under your skin.'

Undoubtedly it is a weird bit of Britain. Crowmere, Denver Sluice, Frog Hall Farm – its place names drip off the map like damp. Water still oozes from every Fenland pore, seeping into dykes and field drains that create endless perspectives with their precise geometry. Yet for all its treeless monotony it is oddly exciting to drive out under the unassailable Fenland skies and see tractors crawling along the horizon, breaking the black earth for the gulls drawn in their wake as if they were following North Sea trawlers.

Travel across it and always it is comparisons with the sea that spring to mind. Even the Fenland towns have the feel of seaports, close-knit havens turned in upon themselves as if unable to face the aching emptiness of the world outside.

To outsiders this unrelieved bleakness is hard to bear. In the Cambridgeshire peatlands – the so-called Black Fen – a single tree can draw the eye. No other English county has so little woodland; yet it was not always so. Even today, out in the lonely ploughlands around Mepal, farmers still uncover massive bog oaks – the corpses of a vanished wildwood entombed in the peat for thousands of years.

These stubborn hulks once spread their leafy canopy over much of East Anglia; but, as the British climate became wetter, the rivers rose and drowned the wildwood. The North Sea had also risen, holding back the Nene, Ouse and Welland that carry the rains of Middle England out into the Wash. Now they spilled across the land, laying down the clays on the seaward side of the Fen, which in turn created vast reed beds in the pent-up shallows farther inland. And as the reeds rotted and sank, generation upon generation, they began to form deep layers of peat.

The Romans were the first to tame the Fens. It was they who dug the Car Dyke, a seventy-mile catch-water drain that doubled as a canal, carrying grain from Waterbeach to feed the Lincoln garrison.

Time passed and the Romans, having cleared most of the water-loving willows and alder carr that had sprung up in the wake of the original wildwood, went back to the sun.

Then came the Saxons. St Etheldreda founded her minster on Ely – the island of eels – and the wind still blew across Whittlesea Mere, throwing up waves big enough to sink one of King Cnut's ships. When the Normans arrived, Hereward waged guerrilla war from the fastness of the reed jungles until the monks betrayed him. And still the great Fenland remained inviolate.

It stayed intact until a group of seventeenth-century speculators – the 'Gentlemen Adventurers' – began to cast covetous eyes upon its unexploited acres. Led by the Fourth Duke of Bedford, who owned large tracts of land around Whittlesea, they sought to drain the peat fens and hired a Dutch engineer, Cornelius Vermuyden, to come up with a plan.

His answer was to bypass the wanderings of the Great Ouse by digging a cut that would carry the winter floodwaters of Bedfordshire straight into the Wash. Called, confusingly, the Old Bedford River, Vermuyden's waterway was completed in 1637, although not without fierce opposition from the 'Fen Tigers' – the marshmen, wildfowlers and eel-trappers whose livelihoods would be swept away.

In the late 1640s, after the Civil War, Vermuyden set eleven thousand men to dig a second waterway running parallel to the first and separated by half a mile of grazing marsh that would act as a giant reservoir in times of flood, receiving surplus water from both the Old and the New Bedford Rivers. Over the centuries to come, in years of heavy winter rains the banks would burst and the 'Bailiff of Bedford' would come to claim his own again; but increasingly, acre by stubborn acre, with dykes and windmills and pumping engines, the Great Fen was tamed.

Today wheat fields ripple where the breeze blew cats' paws across the shining waters of Whittlesea Mere. What was once England's second largest lake is now no more than a ghostly presence of pale marl that shows up in winter against the dark surrounding peat, and the original Adventurers are long forgotten, although their name lives on at Adventurers' Fen, near Wicken. And yet Vermuyden's grand design is still the main drainage scheme for the Cambridge Fens.

To see a countryside shaped by market forces you need look no further than the Fens. Here is a landscape totally subservient to human needs, ploughed, deep-drained, intensively mechanised, where only the wind is wild. In the Black Fen you can drive for miles across a land with never an animal and seldom a man unless he is shut in the cab of a giant tractor, turning over the most bountiful earth in Britain.

'You'll find vast areas without a single farmhouse,' said Jim West of the local Agricultural Development Advisory Service. 'Here the farmers live in the towns, in Chatteris and March, but farm on the Fens.'

What they produce are prodigious quantities of potatoes and sugar beet, cereals and oilseed rape, carrots, onions, leeks and celery. But while half the land at any one time may be under cereals, it is the peat-loving root crops that are the mainstay of the Fenland farmers.

Here as elsewhere, mechanisation and weed control have revolutionised farming. 'Forty years ago, onions were a smallholder's crop,' said Jim Mason, a retired agricultural advisor and an authority on the Black Fen. 'They required lots of hand-hoeing and hand-harvesting. Now they can be mechanically weeded and harvested by machines.'

In Cambridgeshire ninety per cent of the county is farmland – most of it Grade One and Grade Two quality, the kind of land that changes hands for a small fortune. 'As cropping soil it is probably the best in Europe,' said Mike Hollingsworth. 'That's why you rarely see anything on four legs in the Fens. If anyone spots a cow or sheep they stop and take a picture of it.'

But Fenland peat – the black gold of Cambridgeshire – is a finite resource that is wasting away by as much as an inch a year. When drained, the drying peat shrinks and oxidises, literally vanishing into thin air.

The Holmes Fen Post near Ramsey says it all. In 1851 an iron pillar was taken from the Great Exhibition and driven into Holmes Fen with its base resting on the clay subsoil and its top level with the peat surface. Today the top stands a good thirteen feet clear of the ground.

In addition, the land is subject to another Fenland phenomenon known as Fen-blow. 'It happens mostly in spring when the topsoil dries and takes off in the March wind like a black fog,' said Mike Hollingsworth. At such times the wind racing across these exposed flatlands can strip the fields, seeds and all, blocking ditches and roads with drifts of dirt.

In his book *Taming the Flood*, Jeremy Purseglove describes the Fens as resembling 'a gigantic and very profitable grow-bag'. But we approach the twenty-first century in the certainty that the bottom of the bag will soon be reached. On the borderlands where the peat deposits were thinner it is already happening. There the ploughs are biting down into the underlying clays; and all the time the field dykes must be driven ever deeper to drain the land. For the Fenland farmers it is Catch-22.

In the next twenty years the Fens around Ely could lose eighty per cent of their existing peat soils; and as the peat continues to waste away it raises a question that hangs like a dust pall over the Black Fen. What will happen when this, the most extensively drained landscape in Britain, which demands round-the-clock pumping to keep its head above water, can no longer grow the crops that justify the expense?

Worries about the future and the problems of over-production in the European Community have caused farmland prices to drop over the past few years, although they are beginning to bottom out now. Government set-aside schemes to reduce food surpluses by taking land out of production are unlikely to affect the peatlands. They are simply too valuable to be set aside. At present we live in an age of food mountains, but we may be hungry again in a decade or two, making it unlikely that the Fens will revert to reed beds.

Of the old, undrained fen that once spilled across 700,000 acres of East Anglia, only a few tiny remnants survive. The best is Wicken Fen, six hundred acres of sedge and reed beds owned by the National Trust.

Wicken is Britain's oldest nature reserve. Its founding fathers were Victorian entomologists, earnest men with spade beards, leggings and muslin nets, drawn to the fen by its extraordinary wealth of moths and butterflies. Today Wicken stands marooned nine feet above the sunken fields; an island of wilderness in a sea of farmland, its water table drip-fed by a permanent life-support system of raised banks and lodes and drainage pumps.

The glorious black and yellow swallowtail butterfly has not been seen at Wicken for forty years; but in summer the lodes are still bright with dragonflies. The air carries the harsh chatter of sedge warblers, the marshy smells of sweet-gale and watermint. The wind hisses in the sedge, in the foxtail tassels of the drowning reeds, in the leaves of the willows and the alder buckthorn: the ancient sound of the Saxon jungle.

Yet even Wicken is not a true relic of the pristine fen. Its sedge has been harvested for five hundred years and is still cut today to maintain the habitat, as are the reeds, which are gathered in January with the aid of an Italian rice-harvesting machine, stacked into eight thousand bundles and sold to a local thatcher in Somersham.

Ironically the area that most retains the atmosphere of the medieval fens is the Ouse Washes, the winter flood meadows created by Vermuyden when he dug the Old and New Bedford Rivers to divert the waters of the Great Ouse. Vermuyden's legacy is the largest tract of regularly flooded freshwater grazing marsh in Britain. It extends from Earith down to Denver Sluice; a grassy carpet nineteen miles long, half a mile wide and all of it below sea level. In winter, when the tidal New Bedford River is overwhelmed by the floodwaters coming down the Great Ouse, the surplus is channelled into the River Delph, which then overflows, transforming the Ouse Washes into an enormous mere frequented by tens of thousands of wildfowl.

At such times, when flocks of lapwings drift like smoke over the winter fields, the Great Fen comes into its own again. At dusk, Bewick's swans from Arctic Russia beat in to roost with ghostly music in their wings. At dawn the frosty air shivers to the crack of wildfowlers' guns and it is possible to catch the last echoes of that world, not long vanished, of the marsh-men who lived by reaping the wild harvests of the Fens with their nets and traps.

They lived with the damp in their bones, in low-beamed cottages smelling of mud and coal fires, making eel hives, shepherding in summer, wildfowling in winter, handing down their punt guns like holy relics from one generation to the next; weapons with legendary names such as Bacca Jack and Old Jarminy, as venerable as their owners. A few of these old Fen Tigers are still around; but they are the last of their kind.

In January I sat in a hide overlooking the Ouse Washes bird reserve at Welches Dam. The floodwaters were running three feet deep, driven by a bitter wind that hurled flurries of wigeon across the sky. Their whistling voices fell from the clouds, as cold and melancholy as the Siberian tundra from which they had fled. Some winters, said Cliff Carson, who runs the reserve for the RSPB, you might see forty thousand of them on the Washes.

But by March the floods and the ducks had gone and it was easier to imagine that marvellous time in late spring, before the grazing animals are turned out to pasture, when the marsh marigolds bloom along the ditches and the days are loud with snipe and redshank.

Downstream at Welney, in the bar of the Lamb and Flag, a monster pike caught in 1957 scowls from its glass case above the fireplace. The Fens have always been a rich hunting ground for pike fishermen and the Great Ouse Relief Channel offers some of the best sport in Britain. 'Eleven miles of water chock-a-block with pike,' said John Wilson, a tackle dealer, author and television presenter. 'Until fourteen years ago, that is. In the winter of 1976–77 the sluices were opened to relieve the channel of excess floodwater. Unfortunately they were kept open so long that most of the fish were sucked out into the tidal Great Ouse. Their bodies were found by lugworm-diggers at Terrington Marshes.'

But the pike is a great survivor, a living relic from the untamed Fen. While humankind succeeds in driving out the otter, the bittern and the burbot, the wily pike lies low in the slow-moving waters, growing fat on frogs and eels. 'The pike has lived here longer than any of us,' says Wilson, 'and he'll still be here long after we've gone.'

Life in the Eye of a Lazy Wind

Aldeburgh, Suffolk, January 2014

Suffolk lay shivering under a leaden sky, browbeaten by a bitter wind that blew for days, uprooting birch trees on the heaths as freak storm surges laid siege to the coast, breaching the sea defences at Snape and awakening memories of the disastrous floods in January 1953 when more than three hundred lives were lost.

Flooding is no stranger in this part of the world. It is, after all, England's Low Country, and as soon as you cross the A12 and head east towards Aldeburgh you can feel the land spreading out to meet the fifty-odd miles of marshland, mudflats, creeks and shingle spits that lie between Felixstowe and Kessingland.

Here you are on hallowed ground, for you have just entered the Suffolk Coast and Heaths, a much-loved Area of Outstanding Natural Beauty on the outermost edge of England. Its defining features are five reed-fringed estuaries: Stour, Orwell, Deben, Alde and Blyth (Benjamin Britten's Curlew River), each one receding into a dissolving distance whose low-lying hinterlands offer 155 square miles of gorse and heather to explore, together with ghostly glades of silver birch and ancient woods where red deer roam.

Along its shores, at Southwold, Aldeburgh, Orford and Woodbridge, you are never far from a good meal and an open fire. In short, it's the perfect destination for a midwinter break. And that is exactly what I enjoyed – in spite of arriving in the midst of one of the wettest winters on record.

Aldeburgh is an old-fashioned seaside town with one eye looking back over its shoulder to the lower reaches of the Alde estuary. Still trapped in its 1930s time warp, it lies on the way to nowhere, a genteel backwater marooned on East Anglia's broad backside. In Tudor times its timbered Moot Hall marked the town centre, but everything to the east of it has been swallowed up by the advancing sea, like drowned Dunwich, higher up the coast beyond Southwold. Gone are the days when fleets of smacks would sail from Aldeburgh every summer to fish for cod in Icelandic waters.

Today Aldeburgh depends on tourism. Even its Martello Tower, built during the Napoleonic Wars, is now a holiday home owned by the Landmark Trust. But longshoremen in yellow oilskins still winch their boats up the shelving shingle beach and store their gear in tarred wooden huts.

It says a lot for this unique corner of rural England that even on the rainiest days I found so much to see and do. At the RSPB reserve at Minsmere, I sat in a hide and watched marsh harriers revelling in the wind, drifting and side-slipping over acres of reeds. Farther off stood a herd of konik ponies, chunky little beasts with pale suede coats and chocolate manes, brought in from Poland to graze the marshes.

No sign of Minsmere's famous bitterns, but at one point a flock of godwits exploded into the air, spooked by the sudden appearance of a peregrine; and no sooner had the falcon raced on out of sight than a pair of otters emerged on the far side of the mere, rolling nose to tail through the water like a miniature Loch Ness Monster.

Outside again, with a gale seething through the bare oaks, I remembered the words of a former warden. 'Suffolk people talk about what they call a lazy wind,' he said. 'That's too lazy to go round you so it goes straight through you.' But when it blows you come alive and so do the huge watercolour cloudscapes, filled with the constant movement of birds: languid gulls, fast-moving packs of teal and yelping skeins of greylag geese.

To reach the reserve I had driven over the causewayed road that runs from the Eel's Foot, the twitchers' pub in Eastbridge, across a half-drowned sweep of marshy meadows. On either side lay an impenetrable jungle of mossy alders and reed-fringed pools as black as Guinness. Here was an England as old as Beowulf, looking no different from how much of Suffolk must have appeared when King Raedwald ruled East Anglia.

I went to see what is believed to have been the king's last resting-place at Sutton Hoo, on the banks of the Deben estuary. This is a pilgrimage anyone with an ounce of Anglo-Saxon blood should make, leading deep into the long ago.

Excavations undertaken here on the eve of World War II unearthed a seventh-century ship burial laden with some of the most exciting finds ever to grace the British Museum. Among them were swords and spears, a royal sceptre, silver bowls and drinking horns, a heavy gold belt buckle and an ivory purse-lid decorated with gold and cloisonné garnets. But the most impressive find of all was the warrior king's helmet, whose grim visage with its gilt moustache and blank eye sockets has become Dark Age Britain's most iconic image.

Replicas of these treasures are superbly displayed in an exhibition hall containing a full-size reconstruction of the burial chamber as it might have looked when the king was laid to rest.

Afterwards, in the fading winter light, I walked out to the mounds where he and his ghost ship had lain undiscovered for almost 1,400 years. Below, through the pines, shone the Deben estuary, like a dream of the past, whose waters had brought the sea people down from the north, dressed for war with their shining helmets and circular shields, and for a moment, in that silent place with the wind in the trees and the dusk coming down, it seemed as if the intervening centuries had never been.

Later in the week, on a day between the gales when the wind held its breath, I went walking at Blythburgh, whose parish church is known as the cathedral of the marshes. Sun streamed in through its clear glass windows, filling the nave with golden light in which a line of carved angels hovered on wooden wings high above the uneven brick floor, and picking out the scorch marks left on the north door in 1577 by Black Shuck, the saucer-eyed hellhound of East Anglia – or so legend would have you believe.

From Blythburgh I headed inland, following the winding River Blyth through a sea of reeds, then turned off across the grazing marshes to Wenhaston. In Suffolk you can stumble upon the most extraordinary unsung treasures and Wenhaston has two of them.

One is the Star Inn, an unpretentious village pub with blazing log fires and real ales.

The other, known as the Wenhaston Doom, hangs in the church and is a five-hundred-year-old painting of the Day of Judgement, in which sinners are depicted as being swallowed up by a giant fish. Whitewashed over in the 1500s, it was removed in 1892 and dumped outside, where it was due to be thrown on a bonfire next day. Fortunately it rained heavily overnight, removing the whitewash to reveal the forgotten masterpiece of medieval art that had lain hidden for generations.

More surprises lay in store elsewhere. In Peasenhall, the mouth-watering aroma of home-cured bacon led me to Emmett's, a grocery shop whose Suffolk hams, lovingly steeped in tubs of molasses, are exported all over the world.

In Southwold the beach huts were battened down for winter but the Sailors' Reading Room was open, a nineteenth-century mariners' refuge stuffed to the gunwales with model ships and sepia photos of old-time fishermen.

In Woodbridge, the beautifully restored tide-mill that has stood beside the Deben for eight hundred years was closed until spring, but it was still a joy to stroll along the riverside, past houseboats, Dutch barges and a forest of masts with the wind tap-dancing in the halyards.

At Snape, a handsome spritsail barge – the *Cygnet of Harwich* – lay at rest on the mud with her red sails furled; and beyond the Concert Hall at Snape Maltings where the Aldeburgh

Festival takes place every summer, the squat flint tower of Iken church beckoned from a wide-screen horizon of lion-coloured reeds that summed up what Suffolk is all about in a single mind-blowing view.

A Winter's Tale

Snettisham, Norfolk, January 2008

What am I doing here in pitch darkness on the shores of the Wash? Half an hour ago I was still asleep, cocooned in the luxury of Titchwell Manor. Now here I stand in the bleak midwinter, in a wind with an edge like a Viking's axe. Never mind. Soon dawn will come and the bone-cutting chill will be forgotten as one of the greatest wildlife shows in Europe kicks off.

It happens ever winter when, drawn by the imperative of migration, the pink-footed geese arrive from their breeding grounds in Iceland and Greenland. For the last few years, at least a hundred thousand have been coming to Norfolk, with upwards of thirty thousand roosting on the sandbanks of the Wash. There, safe from marauding foxes, they spend the night far out on Bull Dog Sand or Stylemans Middle until daylight comes and they fly off to feed in the surrounding fields.

The RSPB has a reserve here at Snettisham. It's a desolate spot at any time of year, but Jim Scott, the site manager, wouldn't swap it for the world. Especially when the geese are in. Pinkies, he calls them, and he has been watching them for the past twelve years. 'You're lucky,' he says as the sound of the geese comes in from the sea. 'Their movements are unpredictable around the time of the full moon, but they're here in force today.'

And at last we have lift-off. A sudden fusillade of shots from wildfowlers positioned beyond the reserve is the signal for the dawn flight to begin. The hubbub grows, drowning the bubbling cries of curlew, and I can just make out the dark throngs of geese as they rise above the horizon.

They come in packs, the hounds of heaven in full cry, in yelping banners and baying streamers, until their exultant voices fill the air. In flight they make two distinctly different sounds, repeated over and over again. One is a nasal *ung-unk*; the other a higher-pitched *wink-wink*. Repeat those out loud to yourself a few times and you'll be doing a fair imitation of a pink-foot in flight. Then imagine that sound multiplied thirty thousand times – and that's what you hear at Snettisham.

As they rush overhead the noise is deafening. I cup my hands behind my ears and it doubles in intensity. By now it is light. The sun is up. I look at my watch and realise I have been standing here for an hour and still there is no end to them.

Among the massed ranks of pink-feet Scott picks out one solitary snow goose: the joker in the pack. Nor are geese the only birds around. Add hundreds of curlews, thousand-strong flocks of golden plovers and seventy thousand knots and you have some idea of how busy the Wash can be, with anything up to 350,000 wintering birds in residence.

Three days earlier I had been in Suffolk, in the hamlet of East Bridge on the edge of Minsmere. I had fancied the idea of a winter journey and East Anglia seemed ideal; somewhere to walk, to blow away the cobwebs and take in a spot of birdwatching. And where better to start than the Eel's Foot pub, an unofficial HQ for generations of twitchers?

With grey cloud scudding overhead I strode out along the Cut, a mile-long dyke bordered by grazing marshes and pollard willows. The path I followed had been used by the red deer herds that roam the Suffolk woods and heaths. Their tracks were everywhere, leading me past waterlogged tangles of alder carr – an English jungle more than a millennium old.

At Minsmere later in the day I walked out to Island Mere Hide to watch marsh harriers sailing over the reed beds. Minsmere, the RSPB's flagship reserve, is famous not only for harriers but also for avocets and bitterns.

'Bitterns are seen every day,' says Ian Barthorpe, who keeps watch over all the society's properties in Suffolk. Midwinter is the best time to see otters, too, he told me, when water levels are lowered for reed cutting. He also recommended a visit to the flooded fields of the North Warren reserve on the outskirts of Aldeburgh. 'Birdwatching is easy there,' he said. 'You can even sit in the car park on the Thorpeness road and watch the geese flying in.'

Even in the dead of winter Minsmere is a magical place of whispering reeds and shining meres thronged with wildfowl. But to see East Anglia at its wildest you must push on up to North Norfolk. For here, in the twenty-five miles between Cley and Holme-next-the-Sea, lies the loneliest coast in England, an ephemeral world of marsh and mudflats and endless sands where land and tide work watch and watch about.

'Very flat, Norfolk,' was Noël Coward's famous put-down and you can't argue with that. But it comes with an invigorating sense of space and distance that the rest of England does not possess. Broad horizons. Huge skies filled with moving clouds and birds. This is what Norfolk does best; and in winter it is unsurpassed.

Its staithes and villages – Brancaster, Burnham, Wells and Blakeney – speak with broad Norfolk accents of flint and pantiles, white-painted windmills, high Dutch gables and round-towered Saxon churches. Along the coast road its houses and cottages huddle together, tight as barnacles on a rock, as if trying to shut out the unbearable emptiness of the windswept world beyond.

The sea may lie half a mile away across the marshes, but its influence is everywhere. Signs offering fresh mussels for sale hang on garden gates. Others advertise boat trips to see the seals at Blakeney Point. Here and there appear enticing glimpses of silted harbours with yellow sandbanks laid bare by the tide – a reminder that this is also Nelson's Norfolk.

Burnham Thorpe is an unlikely village to have produced England's most famous hero. It lies out of sight of the sea, a mile or more inland, lost among quiet fields. The rectory where Nelson was born 250 years ago was demolished in his lifetime and if it wasn't for the village pub you could drive straight through without knowing he ever grew up there.

The pub itself, a whitewashed building with a rusting sea anchor in the car park, was renamed the Lord Nelson in 1798, and in the previous decade, when he was waiting five years for a ship to command, he was a regular visitor. Today his favourite seat – the high-backed settle in the snug – is still there, along with prints of his greatest sea battles and all kinds of Nelson memorabilia, including original bits of HMS *Victory*.

No wonder most of the pubs on Nelson's coast have nautical names: the Ship, the Jolly Sailor, the Lifeboat. Everywhere except in Stiffkey, whose pub is called the Red Lion – a fitting name for a village whose colourful rector, the Reverend Harold Davidson, was killed by a circus lion in 1938.

West of Cley there is hardly an inch of coastline that is not given over to wildlife or covered by some protective covenant or other. At Cley itself, no longer Next the Sea as its name proclaims, lie Cley Marshes, England's oldest bird reserve, founded in 1926 by the Norfolk Naturalists' Trust. Today it boasts an eco-friendly visitor centre complete with a café and huge panoramic windows, where I sat in comfort with a bowl of hot soup, watching packs of dark-bellied brent geese fly past.

Out in the reserve itself, boardwalks take you dry-shod through the reeds to wooden hides. But after a couple of hours here, watching rafts of wintering duck on the meres – wigeon, teal, pintail and shoveller – I was more than ready to return to Titchwell.

One of the joys of coming to North Norfolk in winter is its welcoming hotels, and Titchwell Manor, a blissful haven of blazing log fires and warm-as-toast bedrooms, is a perfect springboard for this stretch of coast. Just down the road is Titchwell Bird Reserve – you can walk there in ten minutes. In the 1700s there were just fields here, enclosed by a sea wall. During World War II the area was used as a tank firing range; but the great floods of 1953 washed away the old sea defences, and in 1973, when the RSPB bought it for £53,000, it had reverted to salt marsh. Today it is rated as one of the finest chunks of wildlife real estate in Britain, attracting as many as a hundred thousand visitors every year. All its hides have wheelchair access and its gift shop sells more merchandise per square foot than an Oxford Street store.

'Lapwings – my favourite birds,' exclaims Robert Coleman, the RSPB's site manager, as we walk out along the old sea wall. 'Look at the colours on them,' he enthuses. Nearby stand a group of shelduck, resplendent in their bold white, green and chestnut plumage. 'Paint-by-numbers ducks,' Coleman calls them.

Most visitors come to see Titchwell's 'famous four' – avocet, bearded tit, bittern and marsh harrier – but today it's the brent geese that take pride of place. Plump little birds not much bigger than mallards, they are refugees from the Siberian tundra, growling to each other as they whirl overhead in the bitter sea wind.

'People here talk about the lazy wind,' says Coleman. 'But when it blows you come alive. I worked in Scotland for four years and when you are out here on a winter's day you feel you're in a total wilderness; and there aren't many places in southern Britain which give you that sensation.'

We move on briskly past clumps of sea blite. A pack of waders eight hundred strong comes swirling out of the sky to land in one of the shallow pools. They are golden plovers, exquisite birds with black-and-yellow-spangled plumage, and they all stand facing the same way, into the wind. Their voices provide a constant backdrop of sound, a shrill counterpoint to the chuntering brents.

The path ends at the beach. The sea has vanished over the horizon, exposing a linear Sahara of wave-ribbed sand stretching away towards Scolt Head Island. We stroll down through the dunes and scrunch through a wreck of razor-shells left by the outgoing tide. 'They are washed up every winter,' says Coleman. 'I came down here a couple of years ago and found shells piled up chest-high all the way along the beach.'

Norfolk in winter has been a revelation. Bare and sombre it may be; but I have loved the feeling of living on the outermost edge of England. And it still held one last surprise in store.

On my last day, driving home through the open country around Docking, I became aware of geese passing overhead and stopped to watch huge flocks of pink-feet dropping like stones as they spilled the wind to land in a newly harvested beet field. Quite by chance I had happened upon the very spot where the geese had chosen to feed that day. And still they came in wave upon wave, covering the ground like a soft grey cloak that must have stretched unbroken for at least half a mile.

An Owl for Autumn

Berney Marshes, Norfolk, November 1987

November comes to Norfolk with the telltale whiff of sugar beet and an invasion of short-eared owls. Some of these birds may have bred on our own Pennine moors, or even farther north on the peat bogs of the Caithness Flow Country, but most are migrants from Scandinavia.

Of all our familiar British owls – barn, tawny, little and long-eared – the short-eared owl is the least common. Some years the British breeding population can scarcely muster a thousand pairs; but in good winters, in the 'vole years' when prey is abundant, numbers may swell to as many as thirty thousand individuals as they swarm across the North Sea like Viking raiders to harry our East Coast marshes and estuaries.

Every species of owl has its favourite hunting grounds. The barn owl likes rough pastures and water meadows. Tawnies haunt old woods, parks and gardens. But the short-eared owl is drawn to wider horizons. It is a bird of the open country. Moorlands and marshes are its chosen ground and in November, when the North Sea mists close in and the geese return, the short-eared owl becomes the true spirit of the Norfolk marshes, a wintry totem for all those low-lying acres between the Wash and Breydon Water.

Berney Marshes, where the Yare flows into Breydon Water, has always been a good place for short-eared owls. Six had arrived there at the end of October and I went to look for them.

Norfolk lay shivering under an unseasonally early cold snap. At Rockland St Mary the village pond had frozen solid and the wind had an edge like a whetted knife; but the hard weather had also brought the first big gatherings of winter birds. The grazing marshes along the Yare were alive with wildfowl. The bean geese had returned from Russia, and the first Bewick's swans.

Berney Marshes belongs to the RSPB. The society bought them three years ago when the surrounding Halvergate Marshes were threatened by drainage schemes that encouraged farmers to plough them up and grow cereals. Now these surviving Broadland marshes fall within an 'Environmentally Sensitive Area' in which farmers are paid fifty pounds an acre to maintain their traditional grazing lands.

The Berney reserve covers 366 acres of dykes and grazing marsh in a long, narrow triangle between the Breydon Water flood wall and the Norwich-to-Yarmouth railway line. No roads lead to Berney The nearest, the A47, misses it by a mile, but you can go by train to Berney Arms Halt – England's smallest station. In summer Broadland visitors come to the Berney Arms pub by boat and tie up in the shadow of East Anglia's finest working windmill. Otherwise the only access is on foot, following the Weavers' Way down the Yare from Reedham or walking the two miles from Halvergate.

By the time I arrived the wind had died. Breydon Water lay like a mirror, and mist was forming, a grey thickening of air that echoed to the distant thump of a diesel trundling down the line to Yarmouth.

In the middle of the reserve where Les Street, the resident warden, had lovingly recreated fifty acres of flooded fen, the marshes rang to wilder sounds. My alien shape on the sea wall must have startled the wildfowl feeding in the shallows. They rose in a cloud of frantic wings; whistling wigeon, fluting redshank, snipe with harsh, scraping cries.

When the panic had subsided the wheeling flocks fell back to earth in languorous spirals and began to feed again. And only then did I see the ghostly shape fanning over the reed ronds.

In flight there is no mistaking the short-eared owl. In the air it is supreme; a thistledown killer with talons of steel. Wings held in a shallow dihedral, it can skim and glide, or drift weightlessly in the wind, scanning the ground beneath. When hunting, it quarters the marsh with a slow, sculling flight, dropping to pluck an unsuspecting vole from the grass.

The owl turned, flew back towards me and then alighted in the marsh. Through my binoculars I could see its face: a flat mask lit by glaring, gold-rimmed eyes. Lapwings had watched it settle in the grass. Now they mobbed it, diving repeatedly around its head with anguished mewling cries until it rose and flapped away. Later, on the sea wall, I found its pellets: grey gobbets of regurgitated vole fur stuffed with tiny skulls and bones.

Two other characteristics distinguish the short-eared from other owls. First, it is very much at home on the ground. It roosts in grassy tussocks and likes to rest on anthills and low hillocks, where it stands not with the upright stance of most perching owls, but with body bent in a conspiratorial crouch, as if surprised in the midst of some foul deed.

Its other distinctive feature is its habit of flying by day: a hunter of the half-light, emerging at dawn to feed and again in the late November afternoon to patrol the marshes until dark.

An hour before dusk the cormorants began to depart from Breydon Water, flying to their roost on Ranworth Broad. From somewhere out in the mist towards Wickhampton came the distant double crack of a wildfowler's gun. The day was going fast.

Suddenly there came a rush of skylarks and Lapland buntings. I turned to see a dark shape flickering in hot pursuit. It was a female merlin, our smallest British falcon. She flew so low her sharp wings almost clipped the grass as she twisted, checked, dived at a lark, missed – and raced on into the gloom.

No sooner had she vanished than another, much larger bird appeared: a male hen harrier, rocking and sailing on long, slow wings. It was a perfect demonstration of different hunting strategies: the effortless, search-and-destroy technique of the keen-eyed harrier and the furious rush of the little falcon.

Now, in the deepening twilight, the owls of Berney were also hunting. There were three and I watched them floating serenely over the marshes, beating up and down the sea wall, the brimming dykes, the drowning reed beds, until the night closed in and I could see no more.

NORTH

*Behind its walls lies an unchanged medieval landscape of rough grass
and five-hundred-year-old alders, and for at least seven hundred years
it has been home to a distinctive herd of white cattle. In all that time
they have never been tamed and are truly wild, a unique species believed
by some to be descendants of the same animals our prehistoric ancestors
painted on the caves of Lascaux.*

Brian Jackman (*page 186*).

Land of the Steel Bonnets

Northumberland National Park, October 2009

Winter is coming to Northumberland. Down on the coast at Lindisfarne, the brent geese have already arrived from Spitzbergen. Inland, the leaves have turned to gold, piling up in deepening drifts under the trees of Howick Hall. The bracken lies rusting on the Simonside Hills and everywhere from Tyne to Tweed the fires are lit, the scones are baking, ready to welcome any visitor canny enough to know what off-season pleasures await in this emptiest of English counties.

For anyone searching for fresh air and space, Northumberland has plenty of both to spare. A long haul from the south it may be, but how rewarding to recapture the long-lost joys of motoring on near-deserted roads, to go swooping for miles over switchback hills that still have the look of frontier country and feel the past closing in around you.

That is what happens when you follow the B3618 on its way west from Newcastle beside Hadrian's Wall. For nearly two thousand years its forts and mile-castles have lain across the throat of Britain, marking the outermost limits of the Roman Empire.

The view from Steel Rigg sums up the best of it. Here, high above Crag Lough, the hills fall sheer in a frozen wave of Whin Sill rock with the wall on its rim, snaking away towards Sycamore Gap, where the opening scenes of *Robin Hood, Prince of Thieves* were filmed. Look north and, apart from the black smudges of conifer plantations, the rolling landscape of bent-grass moors and boggy turf would still be recognisable to the men who manned the mile-castles.

Just down the road at Vindolanda, archaeologists are still uncovering the extensive remains of the oldest fort to guard the wall. 'Some of the foundations yet to be uncovered lie twenty feet below the grass,' says Patricia Birley, the director and curator of the Vindolanda Trust. 'That's why it will take us at least a hundred years to complete excavations here.' Among the finds unearthed so far are the famous ink-writing tablets described by the British Museum as 'Britain's top treasure'. The originals are now housed in the British Museum but in Vindolanda's own museum you can read the texts and translations of these unique voices from the past. Among them is a letter revealing what the Romans really thought of us. *Brittunculi*, they called us – 'wretched little Brits'.

Close by at Bardon Mill you can pick up the Pennine Way as it hurdles the wall and runs through the Northumberland National Park on its way into the Cheviot Hills. Within the park's four hundred square miles you can see why this is known as the 'land of the far horizon', and its rivers – North Tyne, Till, Rede, Coquet – may be the colour of Newcastle Brown Ale but are England's purest, home to salmon, otters and pearl mussels.

'This is the cleanest Northumberland has been for two hundred years,' says Chris Jones, my guide for the day as we make our way up the North Tyne Valley. 'What we have now is a post-industrial landscape no longer polluted by coal mines and factory chimneys.'

So peaceful now, yet never was a land so cruelly fought over. For three hundred years – until the union of England and Scotland in 1603 – this was Britain's Afghanistan, our own Helmand Province in which a ruthless breed of fighting men rode out with their steel bonnets and long lances to rob, kidnap and lift each other's cattle. These were the Border reivers, skilled horsemen and men-at-arms who owed their allegiance not to their country but to clan and kinfolk, and who became notorious for adding the words bereaved, blackmail and red-handed to the English language.

Their activities also gave rise to the creation of the pele towers and bastles (from the French *bastille*) – fortified farmsteads in which locals and their livestock could hide whenever the reivers came by. Most now lie in ruins but Jones, an archaeologist from the national park's HQ in Hexham, is keen to show me some of the best surviving examples.

Low Cleughs Bastle, near Bellingham, is one. Built four-square from blocks of moorstone, it squats on its hillside like a dreadful secret, roof open to the sky. 'It was still occupied until a century ago,' says Jones. Now only owls and jackdaws live there.

In Elsdon, a moorland village with a splendid pele tower, we stop for homemade soup and scones at the Coach House Tea Room. Afterwards, a stroll across the green to see the church. Inside is the tombstone of a Roman officer, and on the sandstone pillars inside the door you can see where the bowmen of Elsdon sharpened their arrows. The grooves are still there.

More history lies in wait nearby at Otterburn, scene of an epic moonlit encounter celebrated in Border balladry, in which a Scottish army of six thousand men led by the Earl of Douglas was surprised by a superior English force under Sir Henry Percy. In the ensuing battle Douglas was killed, but Percy – Shakespeare's Hotspur – was captured and the Scots claimed the victory.

But of all the Border battlegrounds none is more poignant than Flodden Field, lost among the back roads between Wooler and

Coldstream. I arrive on a day with rain in the air. A stone cross on a hilltop marks the spot and the only sound comes from a tractor ploughing deep furrows in the dark earth in which the blood of fourteen thousand men drained away in a single afternoon.

In September 1513, King James IV of Scotland had crossed the Tweed with a large army. The English, led by the Earl of Surrey, brought the king to bay at Flodden, having made a twelve-mile forced march to cut off his escape route back to Scotland.

And so, on a wet September afternoon, the battle began. At first it seemed the Scots might win, but their advance became mired in the boggy ground. The Scottish pike men sank in up to their knees and were cut down by the English billhooks. In the carnage that followed, four thousand Englishmen and ten thousand Scots died, including the king himself and the flower of Scottish chivalry; and even now, standing among the weeping hills, it is impossible not to be profoundly moved by what happened here five centuries ago.

Next day it is time to head for the coast. Craster kippers for lunch, next door to the smokehouse in which they were split and cured, and a view of Dunstanburgh's hoary old sea castle, its ruins protruding like rotten molars from a shattered jawbone of Whin Sill rock.

Dunstanburgh is dramatic, but is no match for Bamburgh Castle higher up the coast. Begun in the sixth century by King Ida the Flame-Bearer, it soars from the sandhills, the grandest fortress in the British Isles. From its ramparts I can see the low-lying Farne Islands – twenty-eight at low tide, only fourteen at high water – and a snowstorm of gannets diving on a herring shoal.

Just down the road at Seahouses I meet Martin Kitching, who gave up science teaching to run his own company, Northumberland Experience Wildlife Tours. If you want to see an otter or spot a goshawk in Kielder Forest, Kitching's your man. But today he wants me to visit Holy Island. Here in the Dark Ages, among the dunes and deeps and shining sands, St Cuthbert prayed and the monks of Lindisfarne toiled at their priceless illuminated gospels, until the Danish longships drove them out, taking St Cuthbert's coffin with them.

We drive for three miles over a narrow causeway still wet and smelling of the sea, past glistening sands with sinister names – the Swad, the Slakes – and a box on stilts, a refuge for motorists trapped by the tide. Ahead of us Lindisfarne Castle draws the eye like some fanciful redoubt in a Renaissance painting, but right now it's the wildlife we've come to see. Lindisfarne is a National Nature Reserve, a refuge for seals, a haven for thousands of waders and wildfowl.

The wind is as sharp as a reiver's sword blade, but the lure of Lindisfarne is undeniable. The air is filled with the sound of birds – moaning eiders, sweet-throated curlews and skein upon skein of baying geese. And suddenly, as if to underline the essential wildness of the place, a peregrine comes sliding down the sky and grabs a redshank before our eyes.

My time in the north is nearly over, but in a county blessed with huge estates, one last treat lies in store at Chillingham Park. Behind its walls lies an unchanged medieval landscape of rough grass and five-hundred-year-old alders, and for at least seven hundred years it has been home to a distinctive herd of white cattle. In all that time they have never been tamed and are truly wild, a unique species believed by some to be descendants of the same animals our prehistoric ancestors painted on the caves of Lascaux.

To see them I meet up with Richard Marsh, the Chillingham warden, a tall figure dressed in combat fatigues. 'These fellers still think there are wolves around,' he says of three curly-headed bulls glowering at us from under a tree. 'They fight every day.'

Apart from their black muzzles and foxy red ears they are completely white, and although they are the most inbred mammals on earth there is no trace of genetic weakness because of the way they have evolved, with only the so-called 'king bull' siring the calves.

The current herd is ninety strong – the highest number since records began. 'Even so,' says Marsh, 'that still makes them rarer than the giant panda.'

Dales in Crisis

Littondale, Yorkshire, August 1992

In summer, the hills above Askrigg are ablaze with heather. Red grouse whirr on stumpy wings over the peat hags, and from all sides comes the sound of waterfalls and streams hurrying down the steep green fell-sides to the limestone dales below. To anyone from the crowded shires of lowland Britain, the Yorkshire Dales National Park offers a timeless vision of an older, emptier England. In these high, rolling Pennine uplands you can still find space and solitude on a scale undreamed of in England's deep south.

For city dwellers there is magic here, profound contentment and peace beyond belief. The Pennine air is sharp and clean, the rivers unpolluted. In the Dales, in Swaledale and Wensleydale, in Wharfedale, Littondale and Dentdale, old stone barns still stand among the hay meadows. Drystone walls snake across the sheep pastures and every view has its background of huge, bare hills, including the three great peaks of Whernside, Ingleborough and Pen-y-Ghent.

It is hard to imagine a more idyllic part of England. Yet the Yorkshire Dales National Park today is a landscape under siege. It has become a victim of its own popularity, its narrow roads choked with weekend sightseers, its footpaths churned into unsightly quagmires under the trampling feet of the park's eight million annual visitors.

If that wasn't bad enough, eight giant quarries are busily eating their way into the limestone hillsides; and, most worrying of all, hill farming is going through a period of such intense crisis that it threatens not only the farmers themselves but the very future of the park.

Limestone is the key to understanding the Dales. Here is a world of gills, scars, clints and grikes – gritty northern words for gorges, cliffs and fissured limestone pavements of the kind to be seen at Malham Cove. Waterfalls tumble over limestone ridges. In every dale the underlying stone breaks through the sweet turf, sometimes forming spectacular cliffs such as the whale-headed crags of Kilnsey, in Wharfedale. And the whole area is riddled with potholes, a secret underworld of dripping caverns and sunless pools locked deep inside the hills.

The problem, of course, is that beauty on such a scale attracts the crowds that cause congestion, both on the roads and on the footpaths. At Malham, one of the park's tourist honey-pots, forty schoolchildren in bright anoraks are setting out to walk across the fields to Gordale Scar, whose Ice Age meltwaters carved an eerie gorge through the overhanging cliffs. A notice beside the first stile pleads: 'SINGLE FILE ACROSS THE MEADOW PLEASE – YOUR FEET ARE KILLING ME.'

It is a message that could apply to many other parts of the Dales. Although this is the third largest national park in Britain, long stretches of its 1,185 miles of way-marked paths and bridleways are grievously overused. The damage done to the Three Peaks paths is the worst in the country. Every year as many as 120,000 walkers head to the top of Ingleborough, and the summits of Whernside and Pen-y-Ghent also receive at least fifty thousand visitors apiece. The result is erosion on a massive scale. On Pen-y-Ghent the path to the summit is clearly visible from the road a mile away – an ugly black gash caused by the endless procession of tramping feet.

In places the paths have created scars more than 150 yards wide as hikers try to avoid the morass created by an unending mass of heavy boots. All kinds of innovative schemes are being used to heal the wounds: boardwalks, new stone paths, even lengths of matting covered in stone chippings dropped in by helicopter; but the problem remains.

Elsewhere, quarrying is the biggest headache, with more than four million tonnes of rock being extracted every year. Around the huge Swinden Quarry at Cracoe, between Skipton and Grassington, limestone dust from the crushing plant lies like hoar frost on the roadside verges. Above, an entire hillside is being demolished, yet the park authorities are unable to stop it because the Dales are hostage to planning consents given forty years ago, before the park was created.

Nearly all the rock being dug from the Dales is used for road-building or construction aggregate – a situation that sticks in the throat of conservationists. 'What is happening is that we are squandering national park minerals, in this case limestone of the highest quality, and using it to fill holes in the roads,' says the Council for National Parks. 'It's a scandalous misuse of resources.'

Even so, there is still a serene face to the park, and anyone who has ever watched the TV series *All Creatures Great and Small* will instantly recognise this as Herriot Country. Indeed, such is the fame of the Herriot novels that, like the Brontë novels before them, they have spawned an entire tourist industry with its own well-loved Yorkshire landmarks. From Gunnerside in Swaledale there is a wonderful road that runs over the high moors to Askrigg. You rumble across a cattle-grid and, as the descent into Wensleydale begins, you realise that the little grey village of stone-roofed houses is not Askrigg but 'Darrowby' and its comfortable four-star hotel, the Kings Arms, is the one that doubled as the Drovers Arms in the TV series.

Certainly this is still a region with more than enough work to keep a rural vet busy. It's a land with more sheep than people, home of the hardy Swaledale breed. Protected against the Pennine winter by an unkempt grey rug of ankle-length dreadlocks, Swaledale sheep are able to forage on windswept fells where others would find it hard to survive. With their black faces and white muzzles they are as much a part of the Dales scene as the drystone walls and stone barns that grace the riverside meadows, and the park would not be the same without them.

But the farming crisis has hit hard in the Dales. In Littondale one third of the farms have disappeared since the early 1960s. The remainder may have expanded, but not every farmer's sons want to carry on. Changes in EC and government policy have hit Yorkshire's hill farmers hard, depressing the sheep market and halving the value of lambs. Without the grants and subsidies that currently represent as much as forty per cent of a hill farmer's income, many families would be forced to leave the Dales – a thought that makes the national parks authority shudder.

And no wonder: it's the hill farmers who have made the Dales what they are. If they collapse, the park goes with them. In their place, where there is now close-bitten pasture and fragrant old hay meadows, the bracken would soon move in. The drystone walls would fall into disrepair. The stone barns – most of them dating from the late eighteenth and early nineteenth centuries when they provided winter housing for cattle – would continue to crumble. The very fabric of one of the most distinctive farmed landscapes in Western Europe would start to come apart at the seams.

Yet in spite of everything the Dales retain a sense of freedom and serenity long forgotten in the south, if ever it existed. Even to look at a map of the park is to sense the history lying under its skin, in hamlets called Booze and Crackpot, and hillsides that resonate with sinister names: Thieves Moss, Black Shiver Moss, Quaking Pot and Gaping Gill.

This is curlew country, where sounds carry far: the bleating of sheep on a distant fell-side, the demented shriek of tumbling lapwings, and always the sound of rushing water: Hardraw Force falling sheer for ninety-six feet in its wooded gorge behind the Green Dragon Inn; the triple falls on the River Ure at Aysgarth in Wensleydale; Mill Gill Force near Askrigg; Thornton Force near Ingleton and the River Wharfe racing through the rocky jaws of the Strid at the twelfth-century Bolton Priory.

Earlier this year I drove up Littondale at lambing time. All along the dale bottom, daisies covered the lush pastures like fresh-fallen hail. The cries of the ewes and their newborn lambs hung on the wind, and everything that was not green – the drystone walls, the ash trees, the limestone crags and high sailing clouds – was a uniform silvery grey. At Arncliffe a pair of dippers were nesting under the bridge and trout hovered in the ale-coloured pools, reminding me that it was here, beside the lovely River Skirfare, that Kingsley wrote *The Water Babies*; and in Arncliffe church I came across a memorial recording the thirty-four men of Littondale who fought the Scots at Flodden Field in 1513.

Outside, two stoats were chasing each other around a riverside ash. The tree was very old, its gnarled roots driven deep into the limestone bank. Some of its topmost branches had begun to die back, but I could see where black buds would soon put out new leaves, and it seemed then, in that idyllic green and silver dale, on a sunny day at lambing time, to be a perfect metaphor for the tenacity of the Yorkshire hill farmers and their struggle to survive in these incomparable Pennine uplands.

When the River Rises

Derwent Ings, North Yorkshire, January 1984

Heavy with meltwater from the North York Moors, the Derwent flowed under Sutton Bridge faster than I could walk. The river was high and still rising, and I could not see the bottom. Downstream towards Wheldrake it had crept across the fields to form a huge lake from which the bare superstructure of half-submerged willows leaned like fleets of sunken wrecks.

Snow had fallen in the night. Now the air was like glass and an icy wind raked long furrows in the floods that every winter drown the Ings – a twelve-mile stretch of rough carrs and water meadows in the lower Derwent Valley. The wind carried the strange and melancholy sound of swans across the water – not the half-tame birds of lakes in city parks, but Bewick's swans, wild birds from Siberia, for whom these brimming washlands are a vital refuge.

Against the light, in cold sunshine, the water was as blue as the sea, its bright surface beaded with rafts of ducks, its furthest edges flecked with white where the swans were riding. I counted them through binoculars: about ninety of them, together with thirty greylag geese and a mixed bag of wigeon and pochard with a scattering of teal and mallard.

Fifteen miles to the south, the tower of Drax B power station raked the sky, four times the height of York Minster. To the east, the distant Wolds gleamed white against the dark snow clouds. There it had snowed steadily until dawn; but the Ings felt no more than a few brief flurries that now lay light as frost among the wind-blown tussocks.

The Derwent is a remarkable stream. Its waters are said to be the cleanest of any lowland river in Britain; and in summer, when it is not laden with silt, it runs gin-clear between its grassy banks. There are still kingfishers here, and more than thirty kinds of freshwater fish, including salmon and trout, chub, pike, barbel and perhaps even one or two of that all-but-vanished river cod, the burbot.

But the Derwent's real glories are its broad lower reaches, and the Ings that form one of the North Country's last great wetlands. Over the centuries, generations of farmers have installed a system of cloughs, or dykes, to carry away the floodwaters when the river falls in spring, but the land itself has never felt the bite of the plough. Instead its silt-rich meadows have continued to produce a flush of hay so tall, old farmers used to say, that it would brush a horse's ears.

It is a way of farming that has created harmony between man and marsh. It allows marsh orchids and rare water plants to flourish. It provides a hunting ground for otters and barn owls; and in spring, when the floods recede, it becomes a haven for breeding waders almost without equal in lowland Britain. Then the tall grass is shot through with the glitter of marsh marigolds, followed by pink waves of ragged robin and the darker crimson heads of the great burnet.

If allowed to continue, the Ings might go on producing summer hay and supporting winter swans forever; a linear oasis of wet meadows acclaimed by the Nature Conservancy Council as an internationally important Site of Special Scientific Interest. But midway through the 1970s progress finally broke the spell that had held the Ings intact for a millennium: the Yorkshire Water Authority built a barrage across the mouth of the Derwent at Barmby to extract drinking water.

In the following winters the floods lay longer on the land, and some hay crops were ruined. Farmers blamed the barrage; the water authorities blamed the weather. Whatever the reason, there is no doubt that the Ings have become wetter since the barrage was built, and the shadow of a drainage scheme has hung over the valley ever since. Conservationists fear it could be the beginning of the end for these relic wetlands; though meanwhile the farmers still keep to the old ways, cutting the hay in June and then grazing cattle on the aftermath until the silt-enriching floods return.

A magical part of England, then, at all times of the year; but winter is when the Ings come into their own, when the river rises and the land goes under, and wildfowl throng the flooded fields. Bewick's swans are now a common sight. Along with Slimbridge and the Ouse Washes, the Derwent Ings have become one of their main winter refuges. Ospreys have also been seen fishing the floodwaters, and short-eared owls are common. I scanned the fields for sight of one; but all I saw were brown hares jinking away through the grass.

At Aughton, lower down the valley, the floodwaters were lapping at the churchyard wall, but the church itself, like the moated manor house closer by, stood clear of the water on a low grassy mound. There has probably been a church on this site since Harald Hardrada and his Viking army were slaughtered by the house carls of King Harold Godwinson, who surprised them not so many miles higher up the Derwent at Stamford Bridge in 1066. The present church is younger by a few centuries, but its squat shape suits the landscape and the low stone tower has a curious carving of a newt on one wall – a fitting symbol for so damp a spot.

Beyond the church, a solitary whooper swan was upending for food in the shallows. I walked across a wild meadow purchased by the NCC to protect the abundance of marsh orchids and other wetland plants that grow there, and put up another hare that raced towards the distant willows. Where earlier floods had receded, the waters had dumped an ankle-deep tidemark of sodden chaff. I scooped up a handful and found it to be a mass of wild seeds, an invaluable food source for wintering birds, and one that would be lost if ever these undisturbed washlands were drained and ploughed.

Later in the day I came to the village of East Cottingwith to seek out the grave of Snowden Slights, the legendary wildfowler of the Derwent Ings. Carved on his tombstone is a mallard jumping into flight as if startled by the boom of Slights' ancient punt gun, silent these past seventy years. Of all the graves in the tiny churchyard, his lies closest to his beloved Ings, whose waters glittered over the wall, just past the Bluebell Inn. The inscription on the stone reads: In Memory of Snowden Slights, Wildfowler, of East Cottingwith, June 14, 1829 – April 15, 1913.

His armoury was dispersed long ago, but the legend lingers in the Derwent Valley. Wildfowling with punt and gun was still quite new when Slights was born. By the time he was nine he had already left school to join his father on regular punt-gunning forays. At fifteen he was a dead shot, a hefty, big-boned lad who thought nothing of walking to Pocklington market twice a week with a sack of dead ducks – a round trip of eighteen miles. In summer he worked as a basket weaver, and when he married he invested all his small capital in the basket-maker's craft. But soon afterwards, disaster struck: a freak winter destroyed his osiers and left him penniless.

Fortunately the ice and floods that had brought him ruin also provided his salvation. Huge flocks of wildfowl came pouring out of the sky to settle among the flooded fields: wild swans from Russia, packs of geese from the frozen east-coast estuaries, and all kinds of duck. Every day during that terrible freeze he lay in his low, grey punt, the hoar frost encrusted on his corduroy coat, creeping like an old dog otter across the misty waters. And every day his great muzzle-loading punt gun boomed out over the fen, drenching the huddled flocks with its deadly blizzard of lead.

And so he not only kept himself and his family from starvation, but also found he was on the road to becoming the king of the Yorkshire punt gunners. Photographs taken around the turn of the century, and now in the Yorkshire Museum at York, reveal him as a gaunt oak of a man, his face deep-etched by the hard marsh winters.

Those were the days when anything that flew was fair game, and Snowden laid into the local wildlife and any other birdlife with a determination that would have appalled present-day bird lovers. You could buy a pink-footed goose for three shillings and sixpence, bitterns were two shillings apiece, kingfishers one shilling and a jacksnipe sixpence.

Once he had got within thirty-five yards of his target he seldom missed. On one occasion he hit twenty-four mallard and twenty wigeon with a single shot, though that does not see quite so remarkable when you look at the artillery he used – some of his guns had barrels as big as drainpipes.

His biggest weapon, a giant muzzle-loader built in Beverley for his father, weighted 140 pounds and had a barrel ten feet long that could throw sixteen pounds of lead shot. The guns were mounted in an open, clinker-built pinewood punt seventeen feet long with a three-foot beam; and when fully laden its gunwales cleared the water by a mere six inches.

Snowden was still wildfowling when he was eighty, two years before his death. His had been a tough, solitary life, lying for hours on end in his punt, often soaked, frequently frozen (once he was found with his corduroys frozen on him and carried home, stiff as a board, to be thawed out by his fireside). Yet he is on record as having said, 'If I had my life to come over again I would still be a wildfowler, but I would go in for it properly.' God help the geese if he had.

By a strange twist of fate his old killing ground, a wild waste of flooded water meadows called Wheldrake Ings, is now a nature reserve, bought by the Yorkshire Naturalists' Trust in 1971 to protect the wintering wildfowl that Snowden Slights once butchered. I walked out to the hide in the middle of the Ings, following the river where it flowed silently past stricken ranks of fallen hemlock. Wrens ticked among the brittle stems, and a wind of Siberian intensity hissed over the fields. In this last hour of the day the low sun poured towards the waiting distance, throwing giant shadows to where a screaming flock of black-headed gulls was gathered. Nearby, lapwings and golden plovers were feeding. Further off were more Bewick's swans with a few greylag geese and a vast congregation of wigeon.

Beyond, in the east, the snowy Wolds shone across the vale, whiter than ever in the evening light, while dark ranges of snow clouds moved down the North Sea behind them. As flight time came, the sky filled with chevrons of whistling wigeon. Out on the Ings the gulls turned pink in the last rays of the sun, until they looked more like the flamingos of Kenya's Rift Valley lakes than the roosting flocks of a Yorkshire marsh.

Singing in the Rain

Peak National Park, Derbyshire, September 1988

Down in the valley the day had begun brightly. Sunlight glittered on the Strines reservoir and there was not a breath of wind to shake the dew from the bracken.

But up on the moor the air was cooler, the first hint of autumn, laced with the sharp, acid odours of upland Britain: peat bog, heather, rock and rain.

The track led up a narrow clough, a winding gully where mistle thrushes were gorging on ripe rowan berries. I had hoped to find a ring ouzel – a moorland blackbird with a white crescent emblazoned on its breast. Instead – albeit briefly – I glimpsed something far more exciting.

Down below, where the pine plantation ended in a wall of green shadow at the edge of the moor, magpies had begun to chatter in alarm. Suddenly a bird of prey shot out of the trees and slid away across the hillside in a fast, raking glide. It was a goshawk, a larger relative of the sparrowhawk: a powerful, barrel-chested hunter revered by falconers for its ability to kill prey up to the size of a mountain hare.

For many years goshawks were rare visitors to Britain. Then, in the 1960s, they began to breed in the dense forestry plantations of the Peak Park. Almost certainly these were falconers' birds that had escaped and found refuge in the high moorland valleys. Here they have established a regular stronghold and would have done even better but for the depredations of keepers and egg collectors. This year, at least five nests were robbed. At another site a hen harrier was found shot in the nest with her three starved chicks beside her. So much for the sanctity of the national parks and the laws designed to protect endangered species!

Eventually the track emerged above Foulstone Delf and wandered away over the open moor past grouse butts, deep groughs (channels cut in the chocolate-coloured peat) and the treacherous green of sphagnum bogs. On all sides, heather spread in a purple stain; and from somewhere not far off came the guttural 'go-back, go-back' of a startled grouse. Although the Glorious Twelfth was now long past, grouse shooting remains in full swing throughout September, and the birds were wary.

Heather is vital to the grouse. It is their bed and board. Beneath its wiry stems they find shelter from hard weather and hungry predators while the tender young shoots provide the bulk of the adults birds' diet. That is why, every year between 1 November and 15 April, the Peakland keepers burn the moor, getting rid of the old heather to encourage fresh growth and create the kind of conditions that favour the precious coveys.

The mosaic of habitats created by moor burning – heather, grass, bracken and bilberry – also favours other birds, among them the golden plover and curlew, whose liquid and melancholy calls are the true voices of upland Britain. Towards the end of September the moors become a scene of dynamic movement as the first winter migrants begin their long passage south from Scotland and Scandinavia. The resident flocks of golden plovers are swelled by numbers of darker-breasted birds from the northern tundras. The first fieldfares and redwings arrive. With them are ringed plovers, greenshanks from the Sutherland Flow Country and merlins from as far away as Iceland, preying on the thousands of migrating meadow pipits, linnets and skylarks.

By now the calm of the morning had gone. Ragged clouds hid the sun and a wind ran across the moor, shaking the sere heads of the bent grass and carrying the thin, high bleat of sheep. A cold front was coming.

Up ahead, gritstone outcrops with fanciful names marked the crests of the high tops: the Salt Cellar, the Cakes o' Bread and a wild tumble of black rocks – the Coach and Horses – frozen on the skyline in their headlong gallop to eternity.

I walked on until I came to Back Tor, at 1,776 feet, where the moors break away to form one of the classic gritstone 'edges' of the Dark Peak – so-called to differentiate it from the limestone dales of the White Peak with their limpid trout pools and green banks of butterbur. This was the Pennines at their best. Real roof-of-England stuff; an empty world of scowling moors, stark ridges and plunging valleys lit by the distant gleam of reservoirs.

To the north lay Bleaklow and the Howden Moors. To the south loomed the summits of Win and Lose Hills. And to the west, across the Derwent Valley, the gritstone ramparts and desolate peat hags of Kinder Scout, hallowed ground for ramblers and bog-trotters and scene of the great mass trespass of the 1930s, when men and women from the surrounding cities – Manchester, Sheffield, Stoke, Derby – risked jail to claim the freedom of the hills.

Now their dream is a reality and the Peak National Park, created in 1951, provides some 542 square miles of open space and clean moorland air for the seventeen million people who live within fifty miles of its boundaries.

It began to rain. I sat beneath an overhang with my back against a gritstone slab and poured tea from my flask, then packed up and moved on. From everywhere came the trickle of water, the sound of peat squelching underfoot. The thickening clouds had drawn the colour from the hills, leaving them disconsolate and indistinct; yet there remained a quality about these lonely uplands, a feeling of wildness and nobility that does not exist in the south.

A mountain hare – a species introduced to the Peak from Perthshire a century ago – jinked away through the heather. In September, Derbyshire's mountain hares are still brown, but in winter they will turn white like their Scottish counterparts.

Farther on, a covey of grouse exploded like shrapnel from beneath my feet to glide out of sight on stiff, down-curved pinions – a moment captured in a thousand sporting prints. The rain fell harder. In spite of my waterproof it dribbled down my neck, soaked my trousers. Soon even the insides of my boots were sodden. I was being driven off the moor but I didn't care, and as I splashed down the brimming track into the Derwent Valley I wondered at the perversity of the human spirit that sometimes takes such delight in adversity and discomfort. If I had known the words to 'Singin' in the Rain', I would have sung them. As it was, the golden plovers were music enough.

SCOTLAND

She came gliding towards me from the east, like some extra-terrestrial being, dark, massive and silent as a ghost, with an aura of the primeval about her. With her great wings angled back like thick fangs, she moved against the south-westerly March gales without the need of a single wing beat but with consummate ease, as if owning a secret of aerial mastery no other bird possessed.

from Golden Eagle Years *by Mike Tomkies*

Islands of the Simmer Dim

Shetland, May 1988

A mist as grim as a Viking ghost lay on the sea. There was no sign of Sumburgh Head, the first landfall after leaving Aberdeen. The Isle of Mousa was a vanishing shadow passed to port as we slid into Bressay Sound with a posse of kittiwakes in our slipstream and fulmars skimming beneath our bows. Even before I could see Shetland the damp air held the promise of land close by – a smell compounded of fish, kelp, peat and rain – leading us by the nose into Lerwick harbour.

The two-hundred-mile overnight voyage from Aberdeen to Lerwick is the longest ferry crossing in Britain. You sail at 6 p.m. on the P&O ferry *St Clair* – known affectionately to Shetlanders as the 'Blue Canoe' – and dock at eight o'clock next morning. God knows what the Vikings thought of their North Sea voyages, with nothing but a salt sheep's head to gnaw on, but the Blue Canoe offers three-course dinners and soft beds in comfortable cabins and, if the weather is kind, the bare hills behind Fladdabister framed in the porthole at breakfast time.

The long passage north underlines the remoteness of Shetland. In Lerwick you are closer to the Arctic Circle than to London, nearer to Bergen than to Aberdeen. Spiritually and physically, the islands remain tied to their Scandinavian past. Shetland place names sound as if they might have been carved in runes, half Norseman's saga, half *Lord of the Rings*. Where else in Britain could you find the Haa of Stova, Dragon Ness, the Geo of Vigon, the Sneckan and the Slithers?

Now, as then, Shetlanders live in the eye of the wind, cast up on holms and skerries among the long arms of the sea, in stone houses stuck fast like limpets to the shores, or in lonely crofts rooted among wet rushy fields and iris marshes. In their faces and their voices is the echo of their Viking forefathers, as distinctive as the curving prows of their traditional wooden rowing boats, the yoals and sixareens that lie so snugly at rest in their nousts above high-water mark.

Five centuries of Scottish culture have washed over Shetland since the Danes gave away the islands as a wedding dowry, but old loyalties die hard. In the seventeenth century the infamous Earl Patrick ruled in Scalloway. He built a castle there and bonded its stones with blood and mortar as he tried to sweep away the old Viking laws and rights of *scathold*, or common grazing. Today the earl's lair lies open to the sky, and modern Shetlanders have even taken to flaunting their own flag – a white upright cross on a sea-blue background.

In midsummer the cliffs are bright with thrift and campion. Lochsides and meadow bottoms glitter with a king's ransom in marsh marigolds, and orchids flower by the roadsides. This is the time of the 'simmer dim', when it never really gets dark, when you can still read a newspaper at midnight and only a few brief hours of eerie twilight separate the long northern days. These are the days when the air sparkles and the green holms lie becalmed in a sea of Caribbean blue. But nobody comes here to lie in the sun, not when the islanders have thirty different words to describe the subtleties of Shetland rain.

Shetland is for those who put a price on solitude, and who value the silence of empty hills and bays above the torrid pleasures of the south. Some come to fish – to spin for sea trout in the voes or hunt giant skate and halibut in the churning deeps beyond Bard Head.

Some come to dive on the Shetland wrecks – on the Dutch East Indiaman *De Liefde*, lost on the Out Skerries in 1711, or the 'Silver Ship' *Wendela*, wrecked off Fetlar in 1745.

A hundred islands, eighteen of them inhabited and all of them haunted by a brooding sense of time long past. On Mousa stands a Pictish broch – the finest in Britain – a drystone tower, squat and kiln-shaped, dripping with history. You can read in the *Orkneyinga Saga* how it was besieged in 1153 when an eloping Viking and his love took refuge in its walls. Nobody lives there now, but on calm nights the midsummer dusk comes alive with the flickering bat-like shapes of the storm petrels that nest between its stones.

On South Mainland near Sumburgh is the great archaeological showcase of Jarlshof. Here, too, lived the Iron Age broch-builders, eaters of limpets who huddled like puffins in round stone houses under the turf until the Vikings drove them out and built their own settlements among the ruins.

Further up the coast, between Fitful Head and Scalloway, I left the main road and walked out along a tombolo, a narrow causeway of moon-white sand between two green bays, to St Ninian's Isle. In 1957 a schoolboy scratching among the ruins of St Ninian's Church had dug up a hoard of Pictish silver. Now its only treasures are gold lichens on the rocks, and the silver shining sea.

Like most Shetland beaches the sands of St Ninian were deserted except for seals and oystercatchers. I searched the shore for otter tracks, but instead of the distinctive five-toed prints found only jellyfish cast up by the tide. Later, with the late Bobby Tulloch, I had better luck. Tulloch was a Shetlander born and bred, who could trace his parentage back to the sixteenth century and had an unsurpassed knowledge of local wildlife. For twenty-one years he was warden of Shetland for the RSPB and, when I met him, he was still living on the island of Yell, only four miles from the house where he was born.

The mist that had blanketed Lerwick on my arrival had gone in the night. The sun shone. The air was sharp and clear, opening up immense vistas of sea and hills and islands, great fleets of holms and skerries reaching away to the remote Ramna Stacks off the northernmost tip of Mainland. On the ferry to Yell I stood in the bows and watched grey seals bobbing in the swirling tide. Puffins and black guillemots – known here as tysties – flew fast and low over the water, and Arctic terns were diving for sand eels.

At Mid Yell Voe we set off in Tulloch's boat, the *Starna*. We were looking for otters, but on the way we stopped to watch salmon being fed in huge floating cages. Salmon farming had become big business in Shetland – second only to North Sea oil – and there was hardly a voe or inlet that did not have its fish pens. The salmon are weaned in fresh water, introduced to the sea pens as smolts and cropped eighteen months later, when they usually weigh eleven pounds. As the pellets fell through the netting the pens came alive with surging shadows. The fish fed in a frenzy, lunging and turning with silver gleams as if someone beneath the surface was swinging and hacking with a broadsword.

We left the voe and headed for Hascosay, an untenanted island between Yell and Fetlar. Its 750 acres were home to at least thirty otters, said Tulloch, and we looked for them along the Bow of Hascosay between Tainga and the Point of the Gunnald, where the turf breaks away in low peaty hummocks by the shore, creating ideal holts and hiding places for these elusive animals.

Otters like to feed when the tide is flowing and fish emerge from their hiding places. The conditions were perfect, but we could see only seals and razorbills. Then, as we headed into the lee of Burra Ness, I caught a glimpse of a flat brown head, the flick of a tapered tail as whatever it was dived, leaving scarcely a ripple. Moments later it reappeared, a fierce whiskered face framed in sharp focus in my binoculars. 'Otter,' said Tulloch. 'A young dog. He'll be hunting for lump-suckers and butterfish in the kelp forests.'

For fifteen minutes we watched him swimming and diving. Then he came ashore, romped up the beach, rolled in the shingle, lay on his back and licked himself dry until his fur – sleek as a seal's when he emerged from the water – had dried itself in punkish spikes.

We left him an hour later, sleeping behind a rock, and chugged on to Fetlar for a picnic on the beach. Fetlar is famous for its snowy owls, found nowhere else in Britain. Three years earlier I had come here and been lucky enough to see one of these magnificent birds, a true Arctic hunter with round yellow eyes, its plumage the colour of ice and rock. But today we had neither the time nor the transport to reach the hillsides where the owls could be found.

Instead, we made our way back to the Sound of Yell, where mergansers were swimming under the cliffs of the rock stack known as the Grey-bearded Man. Tulloch throttled down the engine and we nosed into the wet mouths of caves and chasms where the water lay deep and clear under our keel and the sunlight slanted down into a darkness of kelp. Above us, every ledge held its pair of nesting fulmars, and all around us the tide sloshed and gurgled against the barnacled rocks from which seals watched with soft brown eyes.

In the days that followed, Tulloch introduced me to the rain goose and the bonxie – Shetland names for the red-throated diver and great skua. The rain geese nest on desolate lochans, sitting tight among the pink-flowering spikes of bog-bean, and the bonxies breed on the moors of Unst, dive-bombing anyone who walks too close to their nests. But of all the islands' wildlife wonders there was nothing to match the time spent watching a Shetland otter.

Highland Summer

Aigas, Inverness-shire, August 2007

We parked in the glen where a shallow river ran. A row of alders grew on its banks, as old and gnarled as a grove of Greek olives, but this was no idyllic Aegean scene. A thousand feet above us the clouds were being torn to shreds in the cold spring sunshine, and there on a stick nest the size of an armchair sat a golden eagle.

Through my binoculars I could see it clearly, the hooked bill, coloured slate and gold, and the frowning eyes that glittered as its head swivelled this way and that, keeping watch for its mate to return.

Forget Landseer's portrait of a wild red stag. This is the true monarch of the glens – a bird of prey with a seven-foot wingspan. At full stretch, dark pinions raking the air, it looks like a flying door and its presence underlined my whole reason for coming here. It just goes to show that you don't have to travel halfway around the world to watch wildlife. Not when it is right on our own doorstep in Scotland's incomparable Highlands and Islands. Over the past three decades I have spent more than three years of my life on safari and can honestly say that the thrill of observing our most spectacular native fauna can be every bit as exciting as tracking Africa's big game.

Of all the rare creatures that abound in Scotland, the golden eagle is the most sought-after, the most iconic. But its domain is vast and remote and to see one – unless it is a mere speck in the sky – requires local knowledge. That is why I have come to this glen with a man whose business is built on sharing the wonders of the wild Highlands.

Sir John Lister-Kaye is one of Scotland's most distinguished naturalists. Born in 1946, he seemed destined for a life in industry until the 1960s, when fate took him down a different path to work on the Isle of Skye with Gavin Maxwell, the author of *Ring of Bright Water*, and his wild otters. When Maxwell died in 1969 Lister-Kaye struck out on his own as an eco-tourism pioneer, taking visitors into the hills and glens of Inverness-shire. The enterprise prospered and in 1977 he bought the House of Aigas, a rambling Victorian sporting lodge overlooking the Beauly River, complete with Gothic turrets and a great hall filled with ancestral portraits.

Today, thirty years on, Aigas has become a hugely successful field studies centre, attracting visitors from all over the world. In just one week, without leaving his own six hundred acres of wooded hillsides, John or his enthusiastic team of rangers will show you ospreys, peregrines, badgers and pine martens; and in the heart of the estate at Loch Cuil na Caillich you can sit in a hide and watch the first European beavers to live wild in Scotland for 450 years.

But wildlife is only half the story. The rest is the setting: the space, the solitude and the beckoning hills. Flying up from overcrowded southern Britain, where most of the sand in the hourglass has fallen, it comes as a shock to discover that Inverness lies above the fifty-seventh parallel, farther north than Moscow, in an undreamed-of emptiness of bare rock and heather.

As you pass over Manchester you are not even halfway there, and when at last you arrive, escaping from the stagnant Home Counties air, Scotland hits you like a blast of pure oxygen. Up here the fields look bigger. The trees seem taller. The Highland views roll on forever. True, the weather can play havoc with your plans, but nobody comes to lie in the sun. Instead, what you find is silence, contentment and peace beyond price.

It soon transpires that Aigas is also the perfect springboard for adventuring into the richest wildlife strongholds of the northwest. Nowhere else offers such a range of habitats so close at hand, from the arctic-alpine summit of Tom a'Choinich – the Hill of the Moss – with its ptarmigan and mountain hares, to the bottlenose dolphins of the Moray Firth.

Farther afield, even the Isle of Skye is only a couple of hours away by car, and John was keen to take me there. 'I've arranged a little treat for you,' he said mysteriously. So next morning we took the Road to the Isles by way of Marybank, where a red kite sailed over the trees, and on into the empty hills of Wester Ross.

In Glen Carron we stopped to stretch our legs and spotted four black-throated divers on the loch below. This was an unexpected stroke of luck. Black-throated divers are extremely rare. At most, no more than fifty pairs breed in Britain – all of them confined to the Northwest Highlands. Anchored above their trembling reflections, they were close enough for me to see how their black throats glowed like shot-silk purple when the sun touched them. John was overjoyed. 'In thirty years of birdwatching this is the best view I've ever had,' he declared.

Yet even this sighting paled into insignificance once we arrived on Skye.

There, the 'little treat' John had arranged was a boat trip from Portree harbour, and waiting to meet us was Dan Corrigal, skipper of the MV *Stardust*.

On the way to Portree the weather had been foul, with squalls racing across the sound to Scalpay, and the summits of the Red Cuillin lost in the clouds. But miraculously, as we put to sea the sun broke through, lighting up the giant green cliffs of Trotternish to the north. Black guillemots whirred from the dripping caves. A grey seal bobbed up between the waves, and as *Stardust* rolled beneath the cliffs I looked up and saw why we had come.

Out from the steep green pleats of the promontory a giant bird had lofted into space and now hung on crooked wings above us. Its feathers were the colours of winter: of hoar frost and rock and the old year's heather. Its beak was hooked like a butcher's cleaver and I knew straight away what I was looking at. It was a sea eagle or white-tailed eagle, known in Gaelic as *Iolaire suil-na-greine* – the eagle with the sunlit eye – the most spectacular raptor ever to grace the Scottish skies.

With a nine-foot wingspan it is bigger than the golden eagle, and a very rare bird indeed. Sea eagles were widespread in medieval Britain, but in Victorian times they were driven to extinction by sheep farmers, gamekeepers and egg collectors; and the last pair known to nest on Skye disappeared in 1916.

Their return to Scotland in the 1970s has been a major conservation success story. Reintroduced from Norway to the island of Rum, they have steadily multiplied until there are now nearly forty pairs scattered among the islands and sea lochs of the west coast.

With the eagle still circling overhead, Corrigal fished a four-and-a-half-pound hake from a bucket, popped a wine cork into its mouth to stop it sinking, and threw it over the side. At once the eagle went into a dive, legs hanging, and scooped up the hake in its yellow fists. Then, pursued by a clamour of hungry gulls, it flew back to the eyrie where its mate was sitting.

That night we celebrated with a slap-up dinner at Kinloch Lodge and, if you can only spend one night on Skye, this is the place to choose. Kinloch is the home of Godfrey Macdonald, the hereditary chief of Clan Macdonald and the Lord of the Isles. But more to the point if you are staying here, Claire, his wife, is a famously good cook with a string of cookbooks to her name, and if you want to dine on local scallops, salmon and venison I doubt if there is anywhere better on this side of the Border.

On the way back to the mainland we stopped off at Eilean Ban, the tiny island that lies directly underneath the Skye Bridge at Kyle of Lochalsh. Its Gaelic name means the White Island, and it was here that John had come at Gavin Maxwell's invitation to write the story of Teko, the last of the *Bright Water* otters. With poignant timing, Teko died only two weeks after Maxwell and it was John who buried him on the island.

He collected the key and ushered me into the house in which Maxwell had spent his last years. Today it is a museum, maintained by the Eilean Ban Trust with help from the Born Free Foundation, and the inside is just as Maxwell left it. Even the Laphroaig whisky he enjoyed still stands on his drinks table.

The sitting room is a flotsam of antlers, otter skulls, letters and trophies that collectively portray the life of this extraordinary man. On one wall hang the harpoons he used to hunt basking sharks for their liver oil. On another, Arab daggers, and on his desk, written in longhand, is the first page of *Ring of Bright Water* that begins: '*I sit in a pitch-pine panelled kitchen living room with an otter asleep upon its back among the cushions on the sofa.*'

Today, otters still hunt in the swirling tides of Eilean Ban, but we did not see one. In fact, for all John's insider knowledge, we had not found them anywhere. We had looked for them in the alder groves of Strathglass and along the shores of Loch Carron, but in vain. Even at John's own beaver loch at Aigas we had drawn a blank. We found their spraints (oily droppings) and the bones where they had feasted on mating toads, but the otters themselves remained elusive.

There remained one last chance – a quick dash to the Beauly Firth before my flight home at midday. So, just as on all true safaris, we were up at first light and off into the crisp Highland dawn.

The sky was cloudless, the firth like a mirror. Downstream at Kessock where a bridge spans the water I could hear Inverness coming slowly to life. In the other direction, fifteen miles away loomed the mountains of Affric, still piebald with snow, and no other sound but the cry of gulls.

A heron was fishing at the tide's edge. Farther off I could see a great northern diver, but of otters there was no sign until a sudden movement caught my eye. First there was one head and then there were three, breaking the surface in quick succession. Then three sleek bodies dived one after the other, followed by three sinuous, tapering tails.

This wasn't just otters – it was synchronised swimming. 'This is what you pays your money for,' John whispered, and for the next half an hour I watched transfixed as the trio – a mother and her two large cubs – romped and roistered through the floating bladderwrack, catching eels as long as themselves and chomping them up with their sharp white teeth.

What my binoculars captured that morning exceeded anything I had ever seen in a TV wildlife documentary. At one point the otters upset a pair of mute swans. The cob bore down on them, hissing loudly, but they ignored him and blithely went on their way, fishing and play-fighting in the sharp spring light as the sun came over the hills behind us and the firth turned to burnished gold and silver.

Rum's the Word

Inner Hebrides, June 1977

When I think of Rum it is not the skirl of pipes that I hear, nor the autumn roaring of the stags. It is the crashing chords of a vintage electric organ galloping through the Lancers in its cupboard under the stairs of Kinloch Castle. Made around 1901 by Imhof and Mukle of Baden, it is still in perfect working order. The only other one in Britain is in the Victoria and Albert Museum – and doesn't work.

Rum by name and rum by nature is this Hebridean island; and Kinloch Castle, built by Lancashire cotton merchant Sir George Bullough at the turn of the last century and shipped from Arran ready cut, stone by stone, is one of its zanier features. To wander round the castle is to make an odyssey in Edwardiana. The greenhouses where peaches grew and the heated pond in which alligators basked are no more, but the rooms are still furnished as the Bulloughs left them, in all their original splendour.

Now the Bulloughs are buried in yet another of Rum's eccentricities: a Greek temple on a lonely shore, fenced around to keep out the Highland cattle.

Today the entire island is a National Nature Reserve owned by the Nature Conservancy Council, and the red rococo castle puts up parties of eager students who come to pore over volcanic faults or hunt for the rare alpine pennycress.

All but one of the island's residents – between thirty and forty of them – are contained in a single square mile at the head of Loch Scresort. The exception is Fiona Guinness, who lives in a shepherd's bothy on the coast at Kilmory, studying red deer. Her only companion is a tame hind, hand-reared three years ago, which has the run of the house and calls every day.

Most of the other islanders lead more conventional, if waterlogged, lives in Rum's average downpour of 120 inches a year. There is no pub on Rum, and nightlife is confined to midnight climbs up the slopes of Hallival to hear the eerie caterwauling of a hundred thousand Manx shearwaters homing in on their nesting burrows.

The remaining forty-one square miles of the island are uninhabited, a melancholy wilderness of glens that haunt you with their silence, of peaty lochans and brooding mountains – the Rum Cuillin – whose dark summits still bear the names given to them by Viking helmsmen: Askival, Ruinsival and Trollaval.

The Rum Cuillin are the worn-down hulks of Eocene volcanoes whose dizzy crags and ridges are well known to climbers. Their most formidable pitches have names like Helen's Horror and Avalanche Avenue. Another is called the Archangel. 'Spread wings of faith and take a short, bold flight across the gap,' says one guidebook.

During my brief aquatic idyll on Rum I shared digs with a genial climber from Torridon called Charlie Rose. He had come to recce the Cuillin for a mountaineering film. Alas for poor Charlie, it rained every day and I don't think he got above five hundred feet in the swirling cloud.

So what else does Rum have? It has its own colony of scimitar-horned wild goats that live on the sea cliffs. It has its own unique breed of dun ponies, sired by survivors of an Armada shipwreck, and its own herd of Highland cattle. In transit to Rum through Mallaig a few years ago, they escaped and ran wild through the streets, turning the sleepy fishing port into a Scottish Pamplona.

There are seals and otters, orchids, eagles and 1,500 red deer. And there are the midges, microscopic vampires that gather by the million every summer on a ravening quest for human blood. On Rum there are days when they darken the skies. They are so voracious that islanders get up at 5 a.m. to dig their gardens while the midges are sleeping. As the local saying goes: kill a midge on Rum and thousands will come to the funeral.

But in spite of the rain and the midges it is a magnificent island: rugged, remote, roadless, Rum.

Dodging the Bonxies

Hermaness, Shetland, August 1988

In August the heather is in flower on the hills of Hermaness and crowberries are ripening in these last golden days of the northern summer. Already the puffins, razorbills and black guillemots have left the cliffs; but offshore it is a good time for whale-watchers, with occasional sightings of pilot whales, lesser rorquals, Risso's dolphins and sometimes a pod of killer whales terrifying the local seals.

Hermaness is about as far north as you can go in Britain. It lies at the tip of the island of Unst: a windswept moorland peninsula bounded by spectacular cliffs and awesome stacks with sinister names: the Greing, the Gord, the Frand. A mile offshore is the beckoning outline of Muckle Flugga and its lighthouse, then nothing but ocean to the Arctic Circle.

The Hermaness cliffs are one of Europe's finest seabird strongholds. At the top are the puffins that breed in their thousands in burrows beneath the turf. At the bottom, the shags and razorbills that nest on the rocks. In between, sixteen thousand pairs of guillemots stand shoulder to shoulder on dizzy ledges, between cliffs and stacks smothered in gannets, fulmars and flurries of kittiwakes. In the breeding season the henhouse reek of their guano-spattered tenements is almost overpowering, and the noise deafening, an incessant shrieking, growling and caterwauling that all but drowns the thunder of the restless sea six hundred feet below.

Yet even this extraordinary spectacle is upstaged by the presence of another, more sinister visitor. In summer Hermaness is bandit country, home of the bonxie or great skua – a bird so aggressive it will fly straight at the head of anyone who dares to walk through its breeding territory. The Arctic skua, a more elegant bird with white underparts, shares the same Shetland airspace; but pride of place goes to the bullying bonxie.

The North Sea is home to sixty per cent of the world's great skuas and Shetland is one of their major strongholds, with at least 640 pairs breeding on Hermaness. In the 1860s it was a different story. Egg collectors had reduced their numbers to a handful of pairs when a local landowner decided to protect them and hired a man to guard their nests. Later, the RSPB took over, and today Hermaness is a National Nature Reserve with fourteen species of breeding seabirds.

The bonxies arrive in late May to stake out their territories on the rough moorland and sphagnum bog above the cliffs. By early June each nest – a shallow scrape in the heather – contains two big brown eggs, and the sky overhead is alive with menacing wings.

Now begins the time when the adult skuas are at their most malevolent. Muttering derisively down their nostrils, they hurl themselves like boomerangs at your head. Sometimes they deliver a buffet with their trailing feet – a blow strong enough to make you see stars – and I defy anyone not to flinch as their avenging shapes scythe past your ears.

The bonxie lives by piracy and murder. A large, brown, gull-like bird with a cruel black bill, it is a nest robber, filching eggs, snatching chicks and ambushing puffins as they emerge from their burrows. It has even been known to kill adult black-backed gulls; but it obtains most of its food by intimidation. The bonxie simply mugs its victims and steals their catch. Sometimes it will drop on a surfacing shag, grab it by the scruff of the neck and hold it under until, in desperation, the shag disgorges the fish it has just caught.

Mostly, though, the bonxie preys on the gannets whose numbers at Hermaness have increased from a handful to more than five thousand breeding pairs. Gannets are wanderers of the wide oceans, wintering as far away as the coasts of West Africa; but in late March they return to breed on Hermaness. Every day the adults leave the cliffs and set out for their fishing grounds up to twenty miles offshore. With a six-foot wingspan they glide effortlessly over the waves, looking for sand eels that are driven towards the surface by voracious shoals of mackerel.

When fish are spotted, the gannets catch them by crash-diving from heights of up to a hundred feet. Their skulls are strengthened to withstand the impact of hitting the water. Their bodies are protected by elastic air sacs and their eyes are placed so as to give them a downward as well as a forward view of their prey.

The great skuas of Unst have learned to leave the gannets alone when they set out on their fishing trips; but they also know their regular flight paths and hang around, waiting for the fully laden birds to return. It is then that the homeward-bound gannets are strafed by the marauding bonxies, upturned by an undignified tweak of the tail or forced to crash-land in the water and give up their hard-won catch. Scientists have a name for the cliff-wise bonxie's feeding strategy: kleptoparasitism; but robbery with violence would do just as well.

Life for a gannet chick is an endless wait for food. For fifteen weeks the young birds must remain on their precarious ledges, in foul-smelling nests of seaweed welded together with guano, their only treat the daily diet of regurgitated fish brought in by the adults who manage to avoid the bonxies' blockade.

Freedom for the juvenile gannets comes in August, when at last they can take to the air, clad in their distinctive grey and white polka-dotted plumage, to learn how to fish and fend for themselves. At the same time the young skuas are also on the wing, refining the predatory skills they will need to see them through the winter as they make the long journey down the coast of West Africa and on into the South Atlantic.

It's the climax of the bonxie's year. By the end of August they will all be gone, heading south on the heels of the gannets. Their departure heralds the end of the Shetland summer. Soon autumn will come with its grey mists, leaving the empty cliffs of Hermaness to sleep through the silence of another long northern winter.

Wings Over Scotland

Loch Lomond, Dunbartonshire, July 2011

Piped awake by oystercatchers on the lawns below, I look out from my hotel window in the hope of seeing Ben Lomond on the far side of the loch; but the mountain has vanished overnight, lost in thick layers of trailing cloud. The Scots have a word for dull days like this. Dreich, they call it; cobweb grey and overcast.

But it is hard to be downhearted when you are staying at the Cameron House Hotel. Situated only a twenty-minute drive from Glasgow Airport at the southern end of Loch Lomond, this is where to come for full-on, five-star baronial luxury. Throw in the Edinburgh Tattoo plus a Hebridean sunset or two and you could fit the whole Scottish experience into its hundred-acre grounds.

The hotel itself – all dark wood panelling and understated tartan – has enough antlers to re-equip a herd of red deer. Log fires blaze around the clock and there's a bar downstairs with more than two hundred single-malt whiskies to sample.

But I have an appointment to keep with a man who has promised to teach me the fine art of falconry. Meet Graeme Neilson, thirty-eight years old and possessed of enough enthusiasm to brighten up the most dreich of days. 'There's no such thing as bad weather,' he announces cheerfully, 'only inappropriate clothing.'

Perched on his gloved fist is Oran, a four-year-old Harris hawk, a black and tan bird with lemon shanks and dark, lustrous eyes.

'One thing I'm very fussy about,' says Neilson. 'I never let anyone stroke my birds and I never stroke them myself. There's no bond of affection between us. Hunger alone is what drives the hawk. Deep down inside he remains totally wild, and as far as he is concerned I'm simply a food source.'

Having talked the talk it's time to walk the hawk, so off we squelch through the dripping woods. Harris hawks are desert birds from the American Southwest, but Oran seems perfectly at home in his adopted lochside rainforest. Crows and magpies mob him as he swoops from one stag-headed oak to the next; but the hawk ignores them all. His concentration is focused on the rabbits that lurk in the waist-high bracken.

Now it's my turn to lure him in. Neilson hands me a leather gauntlet. 'It's only ever worn on the left hand – a medieval tradition that kept your sword hand free,' he explains. Then, from his knapsack, he fishes out a titbit of raw chicken and places it on top of my glove.

'Oran,' he calls, and in flies the hawk to my outstretched arm. He comes at me with the speed of a boomerang and I await the impact, the iron grip of his terrible talons. But to my great surprise he lands lightly on my fist and greedily gobbles up his snack.

Some falconers starve their birds before hunting, believing it makes them more eager to fly; but Neilson disagrees. 'They need food to be on top form. You wouldn't starve Usain Bolt before he runs the hundred metres and it's the same with Oran.'

No wonder Neilson is a happy man. In the brief time we are together I catch the exhilaration of a country sport that goes back to the days of the Saxon kings. 'It will never make me rich,' he says, 'but there's nothing else I'd rather do.'

At the end of the session he hands me a dead day-old chick. It's the hawk's reward for our walk in the woods, and bunny huggers should look away now as Oran reveals his true nature by ripping it into bite-sized gobbets and swallowing them, head and all.

Afterwards, with no let-up in the weather, I opt for a lazy afternoon aboard the *Celtic Warrior*, the hotel's own luxury cruiser. It's a chance to see more of Loch Lomond, the largest body of fresh water in Britain.

On a day so quiet you can almost hear the clouds move, we nose out towards Inchmurrin, Britain's largest freshwater island. The wind has died and the loch is a mirror; twenty-four miles of polished steel stretching from Balloch to Ardlui. At its northern end it is deeper than the Black Sea.

With Ben Lomond still sulking in the mist we cruise on through an archipelago of thickly wooded islands. Among them is Inchcailloch, the ancient resting place of the chiefs of Clan MacGregor, and Inchconnachan, where the men of Luss brewed moonshine in the woods. Their whisky stills are long gone, and the woods are now the unlikely home of a thriving wallaby colony. As we idle back down the western shore the skipper points out the Loch Lomond Golf Course, whose £75,000 joining fee guarantees a degree of exclusivity for members such as Clint Eastwood and Sean Connery.

Next day I set out by car to explore the Trossachs. Known in Gaelic as *an Troissachean* – the Bristly Country – this was the haunt of Rob Roy MacGregor, Scotland's cattle-rustling outlaw hero who was born on the shores of Loch Katrine and buried in Balquhidder. Carved above his grave are the words 'MacGregor Despite Them', a last defiant shout against the outlawing of the entire clan in 1603.

At the heart of the Trossachs lie three magical lochs: Katrine, Achray and Venachar. Each one is buried in dense woods of pine and silver birch overshadowed by the furrowed faces of Ben A'an and Ben Venue, mountains whose dramatic outlines make up for their relative lack of stature. The overall impression is one of unequalled grandeur that no amount of driving rain can dispel. No wonder that when Scotland created its first national park in 2002 it should be Loch Lomond and the Trossachs.

Ever since my arrival at Loch Lomond I had watched with envy as small groups of visitors clambered aboard the Cessna Caravan seaplane moored alongside the Cameron House jetty. Now, inspired by my first steps in falconry, it was my turn to take to the air on a flight-seeing trip. Bjorn Clemence, our pilot, has flown seaplanes all over the world, but loves working in Scotland. 'As an experience it's right up there with the Canadian Pacific,' he says.

As we skim over the loch towards Rowardennan the weather clears and for the first time I see the brooding summit of Ben Lomond. At 3,195 feet, it is the first Munro (mountains over three thousand feet) north of Glasgow, marking the spot where the hard-core Highlands begin.

From the air, Scotland reveals itself as a constant interplay of land and water, shifting cloud and changing light, and I think to myself: this is how it must appear to the golden eagles as they patrol their immense territories; a glorious desolation of forest, moor and mountain crag, of sword-bright lochs and silent glens all held together in a terrible loneliness.

Before reaching the ben we turn west towards the Firth of Clyde, passing the mouth of Loch Long and the Polaris submarine base at Faslane on the Gare Loch; then Clemence tips the plane on its ear and we soar out over the firth itself, over Rothesay and the Kyles of Bute, close enough to spot seals hauled out on the rocks five hundred feet below.

On we go, over empty bays and ruined castles and lush green straths where cattle stand like toys in the fields. Ahead looms Arran, hull down on the southern horizon. Westward lie Kintyre and Knapdale, where Scotland founders in a wreckage of islands, and as we turn again to fly up Loch Fyne there comes a breathtaking moment when the sun breaks through the reefs of cloud to pick out the mountains of Mull on the western horizon.

As we turn for home there is time for one last glimpse of Loch Long running up into the Arrochar Alps with the triple summits of Ben Arthur raking the sky; then all too soon we are ploughing to a halt on the smooth surface of Loch Lomond. It is all over in an hour, but long after I have stepped ashore my head is still in the clouds.

Where Eagles Fly

Ardnamurchan, Lochaber, August 1982

Mike Tomkies does not suffer strangers gladly. In nine years I am only his fourth visitor, he tells me. He is jealous of his privacy. That is why he chose to live in one of the most remote and inhospitable places in Britain, on the wrong side of a loch deep in the desolate tangle of wild hills and glens beyond Fort William.

Home is a croft whose last regular tenant left in 1912. There is no road, no electricity, gas, TV or telephone. His only luxury is water piped in from a burn; his only companion a three-legged Alsatian called Moobli. The living room is a flotsam of antlers, skulls, seashells and eagle feathers. On the desk, a Tilley lamp and a beaten-up typewriter. Here, surrounded by his favourite books – Tolstoy, Nietzsche, Henry Williamson – he struggles to make a living as a writer, forsaking human contact in favour of the golden eagle.

His route to eagle country was roundabout but inexorable. At school in Sussex during the 1930s, his best subject was divinity, but he says he long ago turned away from orthodox religion. 'Christianity demeans nature,' he says. 'Puts man above the animals.'

Interest in the natural world was first expressed at the age of eleven, when he began to collect butterflies. 'I couldn't afford a proper net,' he said, 'so I swatted them with a plywood bat.'

He left school with a burning ambition to become a gamekeeper, but ended up at an estate agent's. The job didn't last, and in 1946 he joined the Coldstream Guards, which led to sentry duty at

Buckingham Palace, boxing for the battalion and later serving in Palestine.

Then one day he bought Tolstoy's *War and Peace*. He read it four times, and one phrase always stood out: 'A good soldier requires an absence of philosophic inquiring doubt.' But inquiring doubt was what the restless Tomkies had always possessed. From then on he withdrew deeper and deeper into the world of books, determined to buy himself out and become a writer.

The first reward for his persistence was a thirty-five-shillings-a-week job with the Chichester *Observer*, where he wrote a column called 'Pulpit and Pew'. Then, in 1955, came the *Daily Mail* and a rising reputation as a crime reporter. He met the notorious landlord Peter Rachman and the gangsters Jack Spot and the Kray Twins. Then came a lucky break. An exclusive interview with the film star Ava Gardner – softened by a week's bombardment of her favourite yellow roses – enabled him to break into the glittering world of celebrity journalism. He managed to meet Brigitte Bardot by saving her poodle from a couple of paparazzi, and thus began a decade of fast cars and endless parties, dates with the world's most beautiful women, jetting between Rome, Paris, St Tropez and Hollywood to meet Errol Flynn, John Wayne, Marilyn Monroe.

It all ended with extraordinary suddenness. At the age of thirty-eight, disillusioned with showbiz and hurt by a couple of broken romances, he impulsively gave away his London flat and flew to Canada where, after toughening his hands as a logger and salmon-boat deckhand, he derived the romantic notion of building a cabin and living like Thoreau in the backwoods of British Columbia.

But even in a forest a man needs money to live, and his inevitable state of financial hardship forced him back into harness as a showbiz writer. In Hollywood his home was the second-hand milk truck in which he'd made the trip from Vancouver, but he earned enough from interviews with Steve McQueen, John Wayne and Robert Mitchum to keep him while he struggled to write a novel.

Back in Canada while he worked, he was befriended by Pappy Tihoni, a remarkable old Scots-Indian who had been born on a dog-sled and who was to teach him the ways of the forest. The novel was a flop, but through Tihoni the tireless Tomkies had become hooked on Canadian wildlife. Sporadic bouts of freelancing and the odd showbiz book kept him going, enabling him to observe the mountain lions, grizzlies, orcas, sea otters and bald eagles of the Pacific Northwest – until one day he found a tattered copy of Gavin Maxwell's *Ring of Bright Water*.

Overwhelmed by the nostalgia it aroused, he returned home and tried to settle in Lakeland, but found it 'too overcrowded'. Eventually he found what he was looking for: an isolated crofter's cottage on a remote Hebridean island. There were no facilities – not even piped water. His fridge was a waterproof box sunk in a nearby burn, his bed a mattress propped up on old fish-boxes. Here he struggled against the unsparing Scottish winters, against loneliness and depression.

Not that he was ever totally alone. Over the years he has shared his solitude with a succession of lodgers: owls, red squirrels, wild cats, foxes, a heron, a sparrowhawk and a carrion crow – all of which have become characters in his books.

When he first moved to his present croft, which he calls Wildernesse, he thought he had made a terrible mistake. 'I walked for six miles into the hills and saw nothing but meadow pipits.' Now, nine years later, he knows every eagle, every foxes' lair and peregrine eyrie within the three hundred square miles of lochs and mountains around his home.

Everything he does or sees is written into his diary. Each observation is a celebration of nature, almost a mystical experience; and yet he is no dewy-eyed romantic. 'Nature is a harsh god,' he says. Only when the talk turns to conservation does a note of evangelism creep into his voice. 'We cannot escape our responsibility to love and conserve what is inspiring and beautiful.'

His latest book, on the golden eagle, is his most ambitious, and is the culmination of a nine-year obsession with Britain's most powerful birds of prey, during which he has logged more than 1,500 miles tramping over the hills.

Cautiously, he has agreed to take me to find his birds. The day is sultry, overcast, the air alive with biting flies. We trudge upwards, the hiss of a burn singing in our ears, leaving the dull pewter of the loch far below. Here are sphagnum and tussock, yellow spikes of bog asphodel, and Scotch Argus butterflies flitting away on chocolate wings as we gasp our way from crest to endless crest.

At first the hills seem lifeless: only the song of meadow pipits seeping from the sky. But up on the skyline we see we are being watched by deer, their ears cocked in V-signs of derision; and when we reach a wild corrie, an immense amphitheatre among the high tops, there is a gruff bark and they stream away out of sight.

Here on the summit, coolness breathes and I can hear golden plovers not far off. Their haunting cries hang in the wind, as sad as a piper's lament. Beyond the peat hags, the nodding tufts of cotton grass, the hills plunge into a glen of aching loneliness. At its bottom a burn winds silver. We zigzag down to scoop its sweet water in cupped hands where it spills through the rocks, then climb another thousand feet to where a sentinel rowan stands guard beside a massive crag.

Across the glen the summits swing away into the high trailing mist, their sullen faces as grey as sleet. And suddenly there she is: the veteran female whom Mike Tomkies calls Atalanta, after the Greek princess of the Calydonian Boar Hunt. A huge, dark shape, claws bunched beneath her, sailing on her seven-foot wingspan towards the opposite hillside.

Almost at once we hear a shrill cry and look up to see Atalanta's eaglet, now fully fledged, lofting out from the crags above us. Tomkies breathes a sigh of relief. Here is living proof that another young eagle has been safely raised. Now we can have lunch; it is 4.30.

Afterwards we see Atalanta's eyrie, empty now, a great stick pile on a ledge with the mummified leg of a red deer fawn dangling in the wind.

The way back is a *direttissima*, so steep at times we have to clutch handfuls of moor-grass to haul ourselves upwards. Tomkies calls it 'the Killer'. He is seven years older than I am, but he still beats me to the crest.

Back at the croft, Tomkies pours me a tumbler of whisky, says we have covered twelve miles, climbed a total of eight thousand feet and he tells me I did well on the hill. I don't tell him I feel done in. But fatigue takes second place to a feeling of exaltation. For I have been to the land of the eagles, to the realm of the high corries and hanging clouds, among the great sad hills and desolate glens, and experienced, albeit fleetingly, the joys and loneliness of this brave and indomitable man.

Stormy Seas and Safe Havens

Cruising in the Western Isles, 1993

With a clap of thunder, as bursts of hail bounced off our oilskins, we slipped from our moorings on the Argyll coast and went rolling out into Seil Sound. The winds were gusting at Force Six, kicking up white horses across the channel, but the *Lorne Leader* took them in her stride. A Brixham trawler from the age of sail, she had survived a century of storms since her oak hull was laid down beside the River Dart at Galmpton, Devon, in 1892. Now, still under sail in this, her centenary year, she seemed to revel in the wild weather of Scotland's Western Isles.

We passed the green islands of Scarba and Luing to port and anchored for the night in Seil Sound. There, after supper, I lay in my bunk, lulled by the boat's gentle movement, listening to her timbers creaking and muttering in the darkness of voyages long past when she trawled for sole and turbot in the North Sea. In her heyday there were hundreds of these graceful old workhorses of the sea. Now *Lorne Leader*, with her black hull, gaff-rigged sails and twenty-foot bowsprit, is one of only three still afloat in British waters, a beautiful survivor of an almost vanished breed.

Between 1910 and 1984 she worked in the Baltic, first as a fishing boat and later as a Swedish sail-training vessel. In 1985 she was bought by Don Hind, her present owner, a Glaswegian ex-merchant seaman, one-time sculptor and veteran sailing master. With his wife Gilly, he lovingly restored her for her new role in the chartering trade.

'She's been patched up, re-caulked and repaired so often that little of the original vessel is left,' says Don, 'but her spirit is still very much alive.'[3]

Now, every year from April to October, the *Lorne Leader* plies among the Western Isles on six-day cruises. Her home waters extend from the Firth of Lorne as far north as Skye and south to Iona, Jura and Colonsay. On board are a crew of five and room for a dozen passengers. Conditions are cramped but comfortable, with hot showers and flush toilets – a far cry from the 'bucket and chuck it' days of the old-time smacksmen. Meals, miraculously conjured up in the tiny galley by the ship's cook, are huge and wholesome, eaten at a communal table in the oak-beamed saloon.

Next morning the wind was still gusting at Force Six, the sea a waste of wheeling birds and ink-stained cloud shadows. The squally weather that had greeted my arrival at *Lorne Leader's* home port of Craobh Haven was the fallout from a vicious depression that had come howling in from the Atlantic and was now collapsing over the Scottish hills.

With drizzle pricking my face like gorse spines, we left anchor and motored out into the Firth of Lorne where, hauling on a

---

[3] In 1996 *Lorne Leader* was brought home to Devon and operated from Dartmouth until 1999, when she became part of the Trinity Sailing Trust's fleet, based at Brixham. There, following a major refit, she was renamed *Leader*, and still features prominently in the Trust's yearly programme of sailing holidays (www.trinitysailing.org).

bewildering cat's cradle of sheets and halyards, we hoisted sail and bore away towards the Sound of Mull. The air was rain-washed, luminous and clear. Looking up Loch Linnhe I could see the snow glittering on Ben Nevis, thirty miles away.

To port loomed the hills of Mull, sombre summits obscured by cloud. Their Gaelic names set my scalp tingling. Creach Beinn (Plunder Mountain); Sgurr Dearg (the Hill of the Red Deer); and Dun da Ghaoithe (the Hill of the Two Winds). Now, as we entered the sound, they provided a dramatic backdrop for Duart Castle, medieval stronghold of the chiefs of Clan MacLean. By the end of our first full day's sailing we had safely anchored again, this time in Tobermory Harbour, where we would spend the night.

From now on every day would be like this. Every morning we would up anchor and be under way by breakfast time. We'd sail when the wind was favourable, motor when it was not, and aim to be at our next anchorage in time for a late-afternoon shore excursion, walking or birdwatching in the hills with a resident ornithologist.

We spotted Arctic skuas, red-throated divers and, once, the thrill of a peregrine hurtling past the boat in pursuit of a panic-stricken oystercatcher; but sadly, we never saw the white-tailed sea eagles that are now regularly breeding again in the Western Isles. Absent from Scotland for half a century, these splendid birds are now staging a comeback after their reintroduction from Norway.

While under sail there would be sudden energetic bouts of rope work as we tacked or gybed our way between the islands under the watchful eye of Nick Clamp, *Lorne Leader's* young Bristol-born mate. He'd learned his seamanship aboard a square-rigger based in Malta, but much prefers the Hebrides. 'The possibilities here are endless,' he said. 'These are the finest cruising grounds in Europe. We may get big winds, but there is always somewhere to find a safe anchorage at the end of the day.'

Just how true this was we discovered the following morning. We had hoped to sail north from Tobermory to the Isle of Rum, and maybe climb by night to the top of Hallival to listen to the unearthly cries of the ten thousand pairs of Manx shearwaters that breed there in burrows beneath the turf. But first we had to round Ardnamurchan Point, the Scottish Land's End.

Ardnamurchan is the most westerly point on the British mainland and notorious for heavy seas when the wind is in the west. Green waves broke against our bows and came sloshing down the wooden decks as we hoisted sail and went plunging out into the teeth of the wind. 'Wear safety harnesses and clip on at all times,' was the order of the day; but as we continued to wallow in the deepening troughs, our skipper, Tim Ebdy, prudently decided to go about.

As soon as he had brought her round she began to run with the sea instead of fighting against it. With the wind at our backs the sails filled in taut, sweet curves. 'She's really flying now, isn't she?' he said proudly. 'We must be making close on nine knots.'

Instead of going to Rum we sheltered in Loch Spelve, on the east coast of Mull. A pair of golden eagles had built their nest on a cliff above the lochside and, as we watched, the male came gliding past, close enough for us to see his hooked beak and fierce glittering eye.

By suppertime the wind had died, but the midsummer evening went on and on until, wrapped in an eerie half-light that was neither night or day, we reluctantly turned in.

Then we were away again, this time cruising to Loch Tarbert on the west coast of Jura. In many ways this remote inlet was the high point of the voyage. Its windswept hills were as lonely as the Falkland Islands, ringed with mysterious sea caves and raised beaches of smooth grey pebbles. Red deer watched us like Apache scouts from the surrounding crags; but apart from these, and the great northern divers in the loch's black waters, we had the place to ourselves.

The evening was golden, the loch a mirror. But during the night the wind got up and in the morning the hills were cobwebbed with hanging cloud. A low front was passing through, said Tim. In the Hebrides the weather is constantly changing: all four seasons in a single day. Sometimes it rained even when the sun was shining, throwing huge rainbows across the water.

On the last leg of the voyage we sailed past the notorious whirlpool of Corryvreckan, the 'Speckled Cauldron', that lies in the straits between Jura and Scarba. In a heavy sea, with the tide running strongly, its roar can be heard more than five miles away; but we passed in slack water when the cauldron was quiet.

We returned to Craobh Haven as we had left, with half a gale blowing and the sky filled with mile-high clouds. But by now we had found our sea legs and begun to understand the bewildering nautical world of throat halyards, bobstays and flying jibs. For much of the time I was cold and wet but would not have missed it for the world.

In the long Hebridean summer evenings the daylight lingered close to midnight, and whenever the sun did appear, transforming the water from gunmetal grey to the purest cornflower blue, we sailed among seas that led like silver pathways under the encircling hills.

In all we had sailed 150 miles and I was proud of what we had achieved. Most of all, I felt the deepest affection for *Lorne Leader*, my home for the past six days, and found it hard to say goodbye. Long after I had gone ashore for the last time I could still feel my body rocking to her easy rhythm.

Hefted to the Hills

Glen Lyon, Perthshire, August 1986

Dressed for the hills in deerstalker hat, tweed jacket and kilt, Bob Bissett cuts a magnificent figure. His beard is of a length that would make Rumpelstiltskin look clean-shaven. With his rifle over his shoulder and a *skean-dhu* stuck in the top of his sock, he has the barbaric air of an old-time clan chieftain going into battle.

It would be hard to imagine a more remote spot than Bissett's home in the Scottish Highlands. His is the last cottage at the end of Glen Lyon, the longest glen in Scotland. The postman brings his provisions up the single-track road from Fortingall, the nearest village, twenty miles down the glen – sometimes stopping long enough to give him a haircut. There are times when no one else appears for days, but Bissett doesn't mind. He and Peggy, his wife, are perfectly happy sharing their splendid isolation with a terrier and a tame goat called Selina. 'She has the same colour eyes and the same expression as that television lassie, Selina Scott,' he explains.

Not that Bob is a recluse. He keeps a visitors' book filled with the names of callers who have stopped for a chat and a plate of Peggy's homemade scones. But most of the summer he is out tramping across the mountainous, nineteen-thousand-acre Invernearn estate where he is employed as a stalker.

Entering his cottage you notice at once the ineluctable incense of burning peat, and wonder if perhaps you have strayed into a Highland folk museum. The living room echoes to the solemn tick of fourteen clocks. A black kettle simmers on the hob, and every shelf and corner betray Bissett's magpie fondness for collecting things: antique weapons, odd bits of brass, books, antlers, animal skins, a stuffed eagle and numerous portraits of Robert Burns, his hero, whom he can quote at length for any occasion. He recalls a visit by a postmaster from Pakistan who seemed fascinated by the picture of Scotland's most famous poet. 'That's Robbie Burns,' Bissett told him. 'Oh, your son?' enquired the postmaster. 'Laugh?' said Bissett, 'I thought I'd burst my kilt.'

In the long winter evenings when the vixens scream in the frozen hills and blizzards dump snowdrifts against his door, blocking the only road out of the glen, Bissett is never bored. He is an accomplished fiddle player who can also make and mend his own instruments; and a self-taught shoemaker, turning out tough black boots with crunching leather soles that look as if they would last forever. But above all he is one of that rare and vanishing breed – the true Highland stalker.

'There's not so many stalkers these days,' he says, 'only killers of deer; hired guns that don't give a damn about tomorrow. The killing doesn't mean a thing to me. It's the getting close, my wits against theirs; that's the satisfying part of stalking. I love to see two hundred stags, with maybe a royal, even a few imperials. But it's not the head I'm after. I'll just as happily take a rogue with odd horns or a hummel [a stag without antlers]. No, it's not the killing. You only get one shot. It's the stalk, and the day, and me pitting my wits.'

He learned his hill-craft from his grandfather. Was he a stalker, too? Not exactly, said Bissett cautiously. A poacher, perhaps? 'Well,' he said, 'let's put it this way. He was a man who knew the hills and the rivers and never went hungry.'

It is a perfect Highland morning, but Bissett is unhappy. 'When the wind is in the east,' he declaims, raising his finger in the air like an Old Testament prophet, 'the wise stalker stays at home.'

Nevertheless, we set out by boat for the far end of the loch, eight miles away, where the great hills close in around the head of the glen. Haunted country, wild and beautiful, but also inexplicably sad.

Will it be wet on the hill, I ask. 'Aye, but don't worry,' he says reassuringly. 'It doesn't penetrate the skin.' But then, he seems impervious to the weather. I am wearing two sweaters and a Barbour. All he has on under his jacket is an open-necked shirt.

At last we leap ashore and march inland for a further two miles, sloshing through a desolation of streams and bogs where exquisite white Grass of Parnassus flowers shine like stars among the rushes. Now the hills tower above us on every side: the Hill of the Castle; the Rock of the Stick; and *Beinn Dorain* – the Hill of the Cold – with its pure springs and rare mountain plants.

Bissett sprawls on his back in the grass and claps an ancient brass telescope to his eye. 'We'll not get a stag today,' he says. 'It's a terrible wind for this ground; there's too much east in it. What you need is a good north or south wind.'

Silence, as deep as a well, and something else: an uncanny feeling of being watched. Sure enough, an eagle appears high over *Beinn Dorain* and sails majestically across the glen. Followed by its mate. 'Aye,' says Bissett, 'there's more eagles than people here now.' It was not always so. Several families lived here once. Now they are gone, their shielings abandoned, the walls tumbled and the land laid bare by sheep and stags.

Again he takes his telescope, steadying it against the haft of his stick, and scans the hills. And there they are. A mile away on the steep green slope where cloud shadows are racing, a herd of deer, sixty-strong and foxy red, are grazing. 'Eight stags, one shootable, the rest all young beasties and hinds,' says Bissett.

I watch them through binoculars. One by one they stop feeding. Now every head is up and pointing in our direction. Even from so great a distance they have caught our scent, and suddenly they're off, hobby-horsing over the gullies until they disappear into a high corrie. 'That's it,' sighs Bissett. 'One whiff of my sweaty shirt is enough for them.' He snaps shut his telescope and we turn and head for home.

There are probably about 250,000 red deer in Scotland and their life follows a regular pattern of movement and migration. In summer, driven mad by midges, they seek relief on the high tops. In autumn the stags roar and wallow on their rutting grounds, and in winter the herds are driven to seek food and shelter on lower ground. The hinds tend to remain wedded or 'hefted' to a certain tract of hill, while the stags live a freer, more far-ranging life. 'A good stag may winter fifty miles away, but he'll always return to the same harem of hinds,' says Bissett. 'I've seen a stag hold the same group of hinds for three years; but after a while he'll be serving his own daughters – and that's the time to send him on his way.'

The stalking season is short: 1 July to 20 October; and the best days usually don't begin before mid-September. This is the time when stalkers earn their keep, culling the herds and taking out clients who pay handsomely to bag a shootable beast. At Invernearn, however, there is no commercial deer stalking, and Bissett's only clients are the private guests of Count Alan Liedekerke, the estate's Belgian owner.

An 'imperial' (a stag with thirteen points to his antlers) is the most sought-after trophy, followed by a 'royal' (twelve-pointer). Bissett himself once killed a huge stag that weighed twenty stone and three pounds – over a ton – but he is a stickler for conserving his stock and will not take anyone near a good breeding animal.

Not every stalk is successful, but his patience is infinite. He once stalked a stag on his belly in full view of the feeding animal. 'Every time he stopped chewing, I stopped crawling,' he says.

Back home in his cottage, we warm ourselves by the fire. Peggy brings scones and tea, scalding hot. The kettle hisses on the hob, the clocks tick all around us. 'I like clocks,' says Bob Bissett, 'but when you're out on the hill there's no such thing as time. You should go to the hill to do a job to the best of your ability and forget about time and not come back until it's done.'

Listening for the Hounds of Heaven

Islay, Hebrides, February 1988

Out of the cold Hebridean twilight falls a wild music. At first so faint I can hardly hear it; a distant chorus of high horns in the wind. Then louder, more insistent, drawing closer until this time there is no mistaking that exultant yelping clamour. It is the hounds of heaven in full cry: a thousand barnacle geese flying in to roost on the salt marsh of an Islay sea loch.

Of all the winter movements of wildlife that sweep across Britain, there is nothing to match the huge migrations of Arctic wildfowl that settle on our coasts and estuaries, and nowhere better to thrill to the sight and sound of wild geese in their tens of thousands than this most southerly of the Hebrides.

Islay is a wet and windy place. The west coast is exposed to the full force of the Atlantic. Only in the woods of Bridgend, where snowdrops lie in deep drifts beside the little River Sorn, is there shelter from the gales. But the sea brings blessings, too. Lagged by the North Atlantic Drift of the Gulf Stream, Islay is spared the worst of the winter. While the mainland shivers under snow, the island's fields stay miraculously green.

Over the years, Islay's mild winters and protection from shooting have led to an enormous build-up of migrating geese. They arrive in October from their breeding grounds on the Greenland tundra: twenty-two thousand barnacle geese and six thousand white-fronts, making this island of lonely bays and melancholy hills a winter refuge of international importance.

Now, in these short February days, the birds must spend every waking moment feeding.

They dig for clover roots, strip seeds from sedges and nibble the salty merseland turf; but nowadays they much prefer the hard-won pastures of improved rye grass, plucking the tender shoots at the rate of ninety pecks a minute.

This is good for the geese but hard on the farmers, whose grasslands are clipped bare each winter. So great is the damage that the eight farmers whose fields are most seriously affected currently share fifty thousand pounds a year in compensation from the Nature Conservancy Council.

Sometimes, when the moon is full, the geese will even feed through the night; but most nights they roost on the sandflats of Loch Gruinart and Loch Indaal, congregating towards dusk to create a spectacle without equal in Britain.

Shivering in the sea wind, I watch them until it is too dark to see. They are such evocative birds. Long after the last stragglers have settled down, their gabbling voices still ring in my ears. There's a wildness about them, and something more, a whiff of the Arctic that makes London seem a million miles away.

Next day, a wild-goose chase to see the birds on their feeding grounds at Loch Gruinart, where the RSPB owns a desolate tract of boggy fields. By February the barnacles have split up into smaller packs, but there are at least two thousand on the reserve this morning.

I sit and watch them from the roadside. The wind hisses in the rushes. A brown hare lollops past. The geese ignore it; but when a peregrine appears, all feeding stops. Up come the heads, black necks erect as two thousand pairs of beady eyes fix on the falcon. Then they are climbing, baying and yapping, heading for the fields behind Bruichladdich.

Above the sands of Loch Gruinart stands the lonely chapel of Kilnave. In 1598 a war party of MacLeans were smoked out and butchered here by the victorious MacDonalds in a bloody clan battle. Now all is peaceful. Sheep graze among the headstones and, in the fields running down to the loch, more geese are feeding. These are Greenland white-fronts – so-called because the orange bills of the adult birds are set off by a white mask. They feed more quietly than the bickering barnacles; but in flight their cry is infinitely more musical, an eager yodelling whose icy echoes prick the soul.

In 1985 the white-fronts were the subject of a major row between Scottish Malt Distillers and the Nature Conservancy Council. The distillers needed a fresh source of peat to flavour the island's renowned malt whiskies and were offered a bog called Duich Moss. Unfortunately for them, it also happened to be a favourite roost for the white-fronts. In the end an alternative source of peat was found and honour satisfied on both sides. Duich Moss is now a forgotten battleground and geese can roost in peace.

A single-track road leads past Loch Gorm, lost in a dun waste of moor grass and peat hags. Hooded crows watch from the telegraph wires like an undertakers' convention, and the sky is the colour of solid slate. Farther on, in a field by the roadside, a couple of choughs are probing the turf for leather-jackets. The chough is a rare bird these days, but not on Islay, where eighty pairs nest on sea cliffs and in the tumbledown walls of deserted shielings.

Back at Loch Indaal the evening flights are just beginning. As the lights of Bowmore begin to blink across the bay, the first packs of barnacles appear. More flocks pour in, turning high above my head, then spilling the wind to tumble earthwards in a rush of wings. By now it is so dark I can no longer make out the tower of Bowmore's round church on the skyline; and still they come, filling the deepening chill with their anguished chunterings.

Later, after a hot bath and a fireside dram in Bruichladdich, the geese still fill my thoughts. Why should the sight of them strung out across a winter sky seem so uplifting? Maybe it is because we recognise them as symbols of something we have lost. Free spirits from the boundless tundra, they owe no allegiance except to the immutable impulse that has brought them south every winter since the Ice Age.

Now they will remain here, feeding and fattening until the lengthening days reawaken their migratory urge. One day towards the end of April the tug of the Arctic will become unbearable. Then they will take to the air in their thousands, calling excitedly as they gain height, and then head north, out towards Tiree, past the Cuillin of Skye, the lochs of North Uist, to be seen no more until they return from Greenland in the autumn.

Acknowledgements

The essays featured in this book span my lifetime in journalism, from the 1970s to the present day. Most of them first appeared in *The Sunday Times* and the *Daily Telegraph* to whom I am deeply grateful for allowing me to reproduce them here. In addition, half-a-dozen extracts also appeared in a slightly different form in *The Countryside in Winter*, published by Hutchinson in 1985. At *The Sunday Times* I would particularly like to single out Christine Walker and Philip Clarke for their unfailing encouragement, as well as Ian Jack and Richard Girling above all, whose sub-editing skills not only transmuted the base metal of my copy but also honed my raw talent as a wordsmith in the process. At the *Daily Telegraph* I would like to extend my gratitude to an illustrious line of travel editors, from Gill Charlton and Graham Boynton to Charlie Starmer-Smith, and also to Michael Kerr and Joanna Symons for their unstinting support over the years.

When help was needed, the UK's national tourist organisations were always ready to ease my way around Britain, as were the local and regional tourist offices, in particular those of Cornwall, Dorset, Northumberland, Somerset and Suffolk. The same support and enthusiasm was also willingly given whenever the RSPB and their wardens were involved, and I will always be grateful for the invaluable assistance provided by the unsung heroes of conservation - the staff and volunteers who work so hard to care for our priceless National Parks and wildlife reserves.

In the course of my travels I met so many extraordinary and gifted people from all walks of life who gave so generously of their time to allow me into their private worlds. Some – Hugh Miles, Roger Lovegrove, Sir John Lister-Kaye at Aigas – have become the closest of friends, but all of them have enriched my life through the adventures we shared.

As for the book itself, I would like to pay tribute to the artistic skills of Jonathan Truss for his superb illustrations, and to my good friend the hugely talented Simon Barnes, a fellow writer, conservationist and old Africa hand for his most generous foreword; and of course nothing could have been accomplished without Adrian Phillips at Bradt for his faith in the project and the unerring eagle eye of Rachel Fielding, my editor.

The extract from *In the Country* by Kenneth Allsop is reprinted by kind permission of Tristan, his son, on behalf of his father's Estate. The extract from *Tarka the Otter* by Henry Williamson (copyright © Henry Williamson, 1927) is reprinted by permission of A.M. Heath & Co. Ltd.

And finally, as ever, my eternal thanks to Annabelle, my inspirational wife and constant travelling companion, who never questions my long hours in front of the computer screen and whose passion for wildlife and wild places sometimes even surpasses my own.